enforcing you

Lisa L. Schwarz

Contact the author:
Lisa Schwarz
www.Lisa-Schwarz.com
www.Crazy8Ministries.com

Also by Lisa L. Schwarz:
Mastering Your Seasons
ISBN: 978-0-692-75960-8

To Love and To Be Loved
ISBN: 978-1-978480-31-5

Discipleship: From Information to Execution
ISBN: 978-1-500192-59-4

Greek and Hebrew word translations taken from Blue Letter Bible.
www.BlueLetterBible.org

Contents

Preface

There are basic fundamentals to almost any concept to be learned that must be mastered before one can go to the next level of understanding. Once that next level is reached, again we find key principles to be mastered before going even higher. And so, the process of learning goes on. Before a person can read, he or she must know the letters that make up the language and the sounds that correspond to each letter. From there, we sound out words. We learn that those words represent things in our world. Once we learn how to read words and we know what those words represent, we move to reading sentences, then paragraphs, then essays. The next thing you know, we are reading whole books!

Likewise, multiplication and division skills are learned only after mastery of addition and subtraction. And before one can move on to Algebra, mastery of multiplication and division must occur. Notice that I am not talking about understanding what something is or knowing how to do it, but rather, I am talking about mastery. Sadly, I know lots of adults who know their alphabet and the sounds that letters make, but they have never mastered putting those letters and sounds together; therefore, they cannot read books. Many know what it means to add, but they have never mastered addition, so they cannot multiply. It is one thing to have knowledge about something—or to even understand something to be true—but it is another thing to become proficient in that skill.

I know what it means to put an Excel spreadsheet together, and if I am forced to, I can fumble my way through creating a basic spreadsheet. Because I have not mastered Excel basics, however, I am in no way proficient in whipping up complex Excel charts, complete with tabs and formulas. If you talk about Excel, I can follow along with enough understanding to keep up, and I can certainly read an Excel sheet, but I have not mastered this program.

You see, there is a difference between having an idea about a concept and mastering a concept. But no matter what we are trying to master, the key is going back to the basics in the effort. My daughter just started taking piano lessons for a second time. She took lessons a few years back for a year, and she knows the basic notes and keys on the keyboard, so her teacher started her in the "second book." However, her teacher quickly realized that my daughter was not proficient enough in recognizing and quickly striking each note as she read them on the staff in that book. Even though she understands the concepts in the first book, she had not mastered them. Her wise teacher recognized that not only was it important to back up but forging ahead would only bring frustration and discouragement. She knows that practicing those basics is necessary in order to move her forward more quickly and effectively into and beyond the second book!

ENFORCING YOU

This book is based on this concept: enforcing YOU. I am writing with the premise that you know that you are created in the image of God and your identity is found in Him. This is a fundamental Truth that most of us would agree with. However, based on my experience as a biblical counselor, this book is also written because many of us have not yet mastered that concept and are not quick nor proficient at walking in that identity. Much like my daughter, some of us need to practice the basics of this truth. That is the purpose of this book... to take a moment, not to "re-learn" what you know, but to practice it so that you become proficient at walking in your God-design.

How do we use the Word of God to realign our minds, our hearts, and our choices with God's? How do we use the Word of God to put a demand on what God says about us and bring it into reality? This book is not meant to simply inform you or inspire you—it is meant to equip you practically. Therefore, I have included an "Enforcing YOU" section at the end of each chapter. These sections not only have Scriptures to reinforce the concepts in the chapter, but also prayer demonstrations to show you how to practice and declare those

Scriptures. Learning how to use the Word as your weapon can be difficult to grasp simply through reading about it and is better understood through demonstration. I have also included declarations that demonstrate self-reconciliation. Many of us reconcile truths with God, but don't know how to reconcile those truths within our own hearts. In other words, it is possible to agree that God believes something about you, but not believe it about yourself, which I explain in my book *To Love and To Be Loved*. Self-reconciliation happens through the way we talk to ourselves. I recommend using a mirror to talk to yourself and convince your soul that His Word is true FOR YOU. That might sound weird initially, but we talk to ourselves all day long in our minds; unfortunately, much of the talk is not God's truth. You MUST retrain your mind to speak love to yourself and come into agreement with what God says about you!

My advice is that you use these sections daily to really start practicing the Word of God. It is my desire that you become proficient in declaring and decreeing His truths, putting a demand on your kingdom identity and enforcing YOU—the "you" you know and have heard about, the "you" you have understanding of, but have not mastered. May you become quick and efficient at reading the notes of life and grow into the mastery of making kingdom music!

Introduction

I was recently asked to speak for a ladies' conference titled "This is Me," after the hit song featured in the movie *The Greatest Showman*. They asked me to focus in on encouraging the ladies to be confident and bold in their identities. I was so excited about the theme because it hits home with what I do daily through our ministry of housing and rehabilitating those in poverty, as well as with my private clients who I counsel or coach. My mantra is "Enforcing Purpose," which speaks of the boldness we must have when chasing down our purposes. For me, there is nothing more exciting and inspiring than helping people discover who they are, their strengths, and seeing them learn how to capitalize on those strengths to enforce their God-given assignments.

Isn't it true, however, that life throws so many obstacles at us, and so many voices attempt to distract and deter us from who we are called to be? Most of us have heard that we must find our identity in Christ and not in the world...but what does that even mean? We nod our heads when we hear the concept spoken of, but what does that look like? How do I get there? And how can I know if or when I am being defined by something or someone other than God? There is so much talk about identity, I think it is safe to say that "how to discover your true identity" has become somewhat subjective and controversial.

I have to confess that I was personally surprised by a fresh revelation from God as I wrote the message for "This is Me." It was a revelation that transformed my way of thinking about who I am and how to enforce ME! It has changed the way I understand not only myself, but also others and their behaviors. I have heard it said, "Change your mind and you will change your life," which is very true. I want to take it a step further and say:

"Change your core beliefs, and
you will change YOU!"

Enforcing purpose speaks of taking charge of what is in your heart (or in the heart of a mission or organization) and bringing it to the surface. It is manifesting what you have always dreamt about and seeing it executed in the way you live your life. But enforcing YOU speaks to taking charge of who you are—your God-design—and manifesting it in the way you act—your personality. It is understanding yourself from heaven's perspective and allowing heaven's principles to become the reality of who you are. When working with people, I have found that before we can hone in on how to enforce their purpose, we have to enforce who they are!

I currently have two messages burning in my heart: this one on enforcing you and another on enforcing purpose. I wasn't sure which to start with and considered writing them both into one book. However, one of them is more from a counseling perspective, and the other is from a life-coaching perspective. Although they are complimentary and necessary, both messages need to be specifically communicated and understood. I strongly feel the concepts taught in this book fundamentally need to be mastered before moving to the next. Therefore, we might say that this book is the prequel to my book on enforcing your purpose.

Once I come to an understanding and full belief in who I am, I *must* do something with it; in fact, understanding who I am should compel me to do something. Conversely, trying to do something can be frustrating if I don't first overcome the obstacle of understanding who I am. Much like mastering addition or subtraction, this book is the foundation to moving into your God-assignment—enforcing YOU—that will inevitably cause you to walk in your purpose!

Chapter One
Your God-Design

WHO AM I?

I don't know about you, but I have spent much of my life trying to figure out who I am. Not what people have told me I am, or who I think I need to be, but who I really am. What—or who—defines me? What exactly is that definition?

Isn't it true that in life, we seek clear, conclusive definitions? Definitions bring clarity; they answer questions and fill gaps. When I am unclear of what a word means, I look the word up. The definition brings understanding to the entire context of what is being said and confidence in what is being communicated. The same is true when it comes to defining people. Defining who we are—whether in life or just in a moment—brings clarity and understanding to any situation or relationship. We ultimately gain confidence and a sense of security within the context of our lives. Isn't this what we are really looking for when we seek the truth of our identity? We want a clear definition that tells us who to be, how to respond, what to say, and how to say it. No variables; just a confident, clearly defined identity to settle the mind and answer the question of the heart: "Who am I?"

I didn't come to know the Lord until I was eighteen years old. His role in my design was foreign to me up until that point. Who I had become was developed over time by the influences of my system and circumstances. My system being my parents, my siblings, my teachers, my religion, my peers, and the culture as a whole. My circumstances being the things I'd experienced (the good, the bad, and the ugly), my successes, my failures, my wounds, and my fears. My life was a sum total of what I had lived on Earth, with no understanding of anything outside the natural. My system and my circumstances were my only frames of reference; they were the only definitions by which I understood all things, including myself. They molded what I believed and why I believed it—not just about life, but also about me. My system was what I returned to when I needed things defined or clarified. Just as you would look up the definition of a word to understand the full context of a text, my system is what I turned to when I needed to understand the context of a circumstance, relationship, or experience. It is where I looked for answers and how I filled in "gaps." My design was defined by my system; who I was, what I believed, and how I behaved were all dependent on and defined by what I had lived. It was all I knew!

The problem was that my system provided an ever-changing definition. It was like aiming for a moving target; just when I thought I figured it out, the definition would shift! I experienced this every time I moved as a child. A new city, new school, new friends, and new teachers brought new definitions with new rules. This led to a life that was wavering and unstable, mentally and emotionally. The world defined MY world. It molded my personality and became the paradigm by which I acted, reacted, made decisions, felt, and thought. After years of seeking to please others and fit in to "my system," I was lost, ever striving to discover who I really was.

None of this is likely an epiphany to you; in fact, I am confident this sums up most of our stories, whether we were raised as believers or not. The voice of our systems is loud. However, there is another voice that speaks; it is the voice of God. Although it may not be as loud, it will always be more powerful! His voice speaks from around you, but most powerfully, from within you; His voice speaks who you really are and stirs up the call on your life.

PREPARED FOR PURPOSE

> *"Eye has not seen, nor ear heard,*
> *Nor have entered into the heart of man*
> *The things which God has prepared for those*
> *who love Him.*
>
> *"But God has revealed them to us through His*
> *Spirit. For the Spirit searches all things, yes, the*
> *deep things of God." (1 Cor. 2:9-10 NKJV)*

We are so good at quoting the first half of this passage, yet we often leave out the part in which we are told that God lets us in on all He has prepared for us. Your purpose has entered your heart via the Holy Spirit. God's Spirit is ever moving within you to open your eyes, open your ears, and stir up your heart to the deep things He has in mind for you. This is the divine sense of purpose that is woven into your being.

> "He has made everything beautiful and appropriate in its time. He has also planted eternity [a sense of divine purpose] in the human heart [a mysterious longing which nothing under the sun can satisfy, except God]..." (Ecc. 3:11a Amplified Bible)

God plants purpose within the heart of every man. Moreover, God's seed contains the DNA to carry out that purpose. God Himself impresses upon you the dreams that you dreamt as a child and the secret desires of your heart. And YOU, your flesh and your "person," are designed specifically and intentionally for those dreams.

When God creates a human, I firmly believe that He starts with a purpose, in other words, a kingdom-assignment. He wraps that assignment in flesh, fills it with a personality (a soul), and then sends it to fulfill that assignment. Think about Jesus. God had a purpose, which was to save mankind. He wrapped that purpose with flesh and sent Him to fulfill it. It was a kingdom-assignment that was literally carried within the person of Jesus. We see throughout the Scriptures instances where a person receives a prophecy pertaining to an assignment his or her future child would carry out. That prophetic word speaks to the heavenly assignment that has purposed the conception, birth, and life of that child.

This should change the way we understand our value! We don't just have a purpose; we have a *specific* purpose that was prepared in advance to conquer. And God set us up for success by designing and molding us around that purpose. In other words, you are perfectly designed for your purpose!

> *"For we are His workmanship, created in Christ Jesus for good works, which God prepared beforehand that we should walk in them." (Eph. 2:10 NKJV)*

This is great news! It means that God didn't just put dreams in our hearts; He also designed who we are to fit those dreams, "that we should walk in them." Like a hand in a glove, so our design and purpose are uniquely fitted and intended to function together as one.

> *"Come to Me, all you who labor and are heavy laden, and I will give you rest. Take My yoke upon you and learn from Me, for I am gentle and lowly in heart, and you will find rest for your souls. For My yoke is easy and My burden is light." (Matthew 11:28-30 NKJV)*

The word "easy" used in these verses doesn't

mean easy in the way we use the term. It means fitting, beneficial, and kindly; as in a benefactor. When we are walking with the Lord, our purpose and assignment fit who we are! You see, this means you can work really hard, but nothing is hard work, because who you are is a perfect fit to what you are doing. That is what it is like when you are living in your "sweet spot." God designed you to be beneficial to your assignment. In other words, you are the benefactor to your purpose.

This is important to understand because you won't walk in the fullness of your purpose until you are walking in the fullness of your God-design. You must love your God-design, choose your God-design, and put a demand on your God-design. This is what it means to enforce YOU!

Once you are walking in the fullness of who you are, who you are called to be will flow out of you with ease. Coming into your design will drive you to do all that is in your heart. Remember that God-seed? The seed of purpose that you carry is watered, fertilized, cultivated, and brought forth as you walk in the fullness of your God-design.

DEFINE GOD-DESIGN

So, what is your God-design? Simply put, it is God's definition of you. While our systems offer a definition, God has written a definition in our hearts; it is an internal definition rather than an external one.

The Urban Dictionary reads: "If you define something, you show, describe, or state clearly what it is and what it is like." Isn't it refreshing to know that God has shown, described, and clearly stated "what is" when it comes to you and me? Our God-design was shown, exemplified, and seen in the person of Jesus. He is the perfect display of the perfect God-design; the potential of man walking in the fullness of the Spirit. Furthermore, our design is described and clearly stated all throughout Scripture. God defines over and over, "This is WHAT IS!" –the definition of you and me!

"... as He is, so we are in this world."
(1 John 4:17b ASV)

Just as Jesus was, so we are! That is the truth of who we are. Jesus is the plumb line of our God-design upon which we establish the integrity of how we define our lives. His life and very "person," the way He lived, the way He acted, the way He responded, the words He used, His wisdom, His love, His compassion, His grace, and His kindness—all of who He was—IS our God-design. He is our fullest potential, our "God-ability." He is more than what could be or should be in our lives, He is WHAT IS. This means "what is" is in you. He was the fulfillment of God's original purpose for man. He accomplished in the flesh what God had in mind all along: for man to live in the image of God (Gen. 1:29). The blood of Jesus reconciles us to that image, that definition. This is the definition of our God-design and simply "what is."

While I really would love to dive more deeply into how we are designed in the image of God, remember, that is not the purpose of this book (that book will come later). The purpose of this book is to guide you to master your God-design and enforce it in your life. So, let's simply agree that it is an established fundamental that Jesus defines our true design, and we will move forward toward mastering that design.

REST IN GOD'S DESIGN

Let's go back to Matthew 11:28-30.

> *"Come to Me, all you who labor and are heavy laden, and I will give you rest. Take My yoke upon you and learn from Me, for I am gentle and lowly in heart, and you will find rest for your souls. For My yoke is easy and My burden is light." (Matthew 11:28-30 NKJV)*

Think with me about how this passage applies to this entire concept of wresting with who we are. There is a heaviness that the world's definition brings that keeps us striving, laboring to conform to the world's view of acceptance, love, and "fitting in." We too often become yoked to that definition, forced to shift with the moving target of the world's ways. We become navigated by the waves of the culture and steered by its opinions and perceptions. There is no rest in being yoked to the world.

Jesus knew that this was the weariness and

the heavy-laden condition that His audience in Matthew 11 were experiencing. They were no doubt exacerbated by the winds of change, as are many of us. Understanding the hearts of those He addressed, and the heart of man, but more importantly knowing the potential of man, He spoke into this issue and gave us the antidote.

Jesus implores them to come to Him and take His yoke upon them and learn from Him. He is saying, "Be one with me! Consider who I am. I am your blueprint. Live your lives accordingly."

This message goes way beyond salvation. It instructs us to find who we are while we are here on Earth. It leads us to be at peace with who we are and find rest in our God-design. He is saying that when we line ourselves up with Him, then we will be navigated by His definition. We are in position to learn from His example, from His personality, and from His life. There we find relief from the world and rest for our souls, our minds, wills, and emotions (our personalities). We will cease from striving and just be; loosing our God-design from within. It will be easy, light, and fitting. I like the way The Voice paraphrases verse 29:

> "Put My yoke upon your shoulders—it might appear heavy at first, but it is perfectly fitted to your curves."

Your design is perfectly crafted to the person of Jesus. As you discover Him, you will discover you!

To be one with Him (who He is), is to become one with who you are.

It is time to release yourself from the world, unlock the yoke, and shut down the voice of your system. Erase the external definition that has been placed upon your shoulders. Run to Jesus and take His yoke. There you will find rest!

> *"It shall come to pass in that day*
> *That his burden will be taken away from your shoulder,*
> *And his yoke from your neck,*
> *And the yoke will be destroyed because of the anointing oil." (Is. 10:27 NKJV)*

> *"When that time comes, all the weight of Assyria will be lifted off of your shoulders; its yoke will be removed from your neck, and the burden of their assault and demands will evaporate, and you'll be free."*
> *(Is. 10:27 The Voice)*

I think it is noteworthy to mention that all throughout the Scriptures, God is defining people. When He gives them a new name, He is defining who they are and what they are going to do. He shows who they will become and what their purpose is! Jesus does this as well. He often said things like, "You are no longer Simon, but instead Peter, meaning 'rock,' the foundation upon which the church will be built!"

You see, just like God, Jesus demonstrated the new definition we have in Him, and with it, we are freed from our past and launched into our futures. Free from the burdens of the world's definition and released into His!

Prayer Practice:

God, I praise You because I am fearfully and wonderfully made. I praise you that I was knit together with a God-design for a heavenly purpose. Thank You that as I yoke myself to You, connect my heart with Yours, and come into the truth of Your design, I find relief and rest from the pressures and opinions of the world. I silence my system in Jesus' name and tune my ear to Your voice. I desire my ears to hear, my eyes to see, and my heart to know all that You have prepared for me. Thank You, Lord, for the ease of walking in my purpose. In it, I work hard, but nothing seems to be hard work. For I am Your workmanship, crafted intentionally to fill the call and the stirrings of my heart. In Jesus' name, amen.

Enforcing You

Passage:

"For you created my inmost being;
you knit me together in my mother's womb.
I praise you because I am fearfully and wonderfully
made;
your works are wonderful, I know that full well."
(Psalm 139:13&14 NKJV)

———————

Declaration:

Father, You created me, outside and inside. My heart,
my desires, and my dreams have been impressed into
my soul by Your hand. I declare and decree that all
that is in me is of You, intended for Your work. I am
not without purpose nor am I without heart. I agree
that while I was yet in my mother's womb, You knit it
all with perfection. Therefore, I will praise You and I
agree that I am a wonderful work. I speak to my soul
and I call myself into alignment with the truth that I
am made with intention and great wonder.

———————

Self-reconciliation:

[Say your name], God created you personally and
intimately. There is not part of you that is not filled
with wonder and beauty. I stand in awe of your God-
design! You have a purpose that was woven into you
while you were not yet born and that purpose is a
part of you and carries value for the kingdom.

Passage:

"So God created mankind in his own image, in the image of God he created them; male and female he created them." (Genesis 1:27 NKJV)

Declaration:

God, I am created in Your image. The beauty of You is in me, and my life is a reflection of You.

Self-reconciliation:

[Say your name], you are created in the image of God and your life reflects Him in all things!

Passage:

"... as He is, so we are in this world."
(1 John 4:17b NKJV)

Declaration:

Father, Just as You are, so I am here on earth. I agree with the beauty of my creation and my image. With the same countenance that Jesus lived, so I also live. I desire Your love, oh God, to flow freely through me in Jesus' name; I desire the power of Jesus to be freely seen in all I am. Thank You for manifesting Your character in me.

21

Self-reconciliation:

[Say your name], you are a beautiful and fine creation of God. You bear the image of God! Just as Jesus was, so you are, here in this world. The countenance of God is upon you and your face manifests His character and love.

Passage:

"And as we have borne the image of the man of dust, we shall also bear the image of the heavenly Man." (1 Cor. 15:49 NKJV)

Declaration:

Just as easily as I bear the likeness of my parents, so I also bear the likeness of Jesus.

Self-reconciliation:

[Say your name], you look like your parents in the flesh, but your spirit looks like Jesus! When you look in the mirror, you no longer see what is of this earth; with spiritual eyes, you see the design of Jesus woven into your being.

Passage:

"But we all, with unveiled face, beholding as in a mirror the glory of the Lord, are being transformed into the same image from glory to glory, just as by the Spirit of the Lord." (1 Cor. 3:18 NKJV)

Declaration:

I praise You that my face is no longer veiled, but that Your glory is seen in me. I praise You that I have no need to cover my identity because my likeness of You is not fading, it is growing, day after day, and by Your Spirit, I am looking more like You. I am on the increase!

Self-reconciliation:

[Say your name], there is an organic growth of Jesus taking place in you. Every day you are looking and acting more like Him. You are growing in your walk and your very being is expanding with the likeness of the kingdom. You are designed to increase with Him, and you are increasing!

Passage:

"For we are His workmanship, created in Christ Jesus for good works, which God prepared beforehand that we should walk in them." (Eph. 2:10 NKJV)

Declaration:

Father, I agree that I am Your workmanship and that I was crafted and designed by Your hand. I declare that I am crafted with purpose, for a good purpose that carries value. I declare that I have been equipped to walk in that purpose.

Self-reconciliation:

[Say your name], you are the work of God. He crafted your design for a specific purpose, and it is good and valuable. You are not ill-equipped. The Spirit of the Living God fills you with all you need to reflect your God-design and walk in your God-purpose.

Chapter Two
Core Beliefs

Now that we have spent some time establishing some basic truths about who we are and the definition of our design, let's start moving forward on enforcing you. Chances are that much of the information I have given so far is not breaking news to you, yet chances also are that you still aren't walking in the reality of that information. My first book, *Discipleship: From Information to Execution*, is all about teaching people how to move beyond knowledge and into reality. There is one thing that keeps information from becoming reality and that is your action. Here is some good news: God has given you the authority to navigate reality in your life. This book is all about enforcing you; understanding that there is an establishment that has already been accomplished that simply needs to be enforced. I wrestled with a title that would remind you that although there is an action you need to engage in to bring the "real you" to the surface, it is not something that needs to be worked for. It is about understanding a core truth and then putting a demand on it to enforce YOU to rise up!

Let's talk more about core truths in our lives. Within every heart and mind, there are core beliefs about life, about politics, about relationships, about work—about everything! But let's focus on the core beliefs you have about yourself. In other words, within your own heart and mind, you have core beliefs about yourself. Remember, as I stated in the first chapter, the system that you have been exposed to throughout life (your experiences and the reality of how you have lived) has become the paradigm that has developed your pattern of thinking, feeling, and living. It navigates your thoughts, your feelings, and your choices. These things ultimately shape your personality. The paradigm *around* you molds the paradigm *within* you. Remember, your system becomes your frame of reference by which you define things. You pull from what you know and have experienced to gain understanding and seek answers. In other words, the pattern or paradigm of the world ends up molding your core beliefs... not just about life, but also about what you believe about yourself!

But where is God in that? If we are not intentional to ground ourselves in the foundation of Jesus, then we will find ourselves building upon the world's ideals and definitions.

> *"As you therefore have received Christ Jesus the Lord, so walk in Him, rooted and built up in Him and established in the faith, as you have been taught, abounding in it with thanksgiving.*

> *"Beware lest anyone cheat you through*

philosophy and empty deceit, according to the tradition of men, according to the basic principles of the world, and not according to Christ. For in Him dwells all the fullness of the Godhead bodily; and you are complete in Him, who is the head of all principality and power." (Col. 2:6-10 NKJV)

Let's break this passage down as it holds some fundamental truths that we need to grab a hold of! This passage gives an invitation, then a warning, and then a reward.

THE INVITATION

"As you therefore have received Christ Jesus the Lord, so walk in Him, rooted and built up in Him and established in the faith, as you have been taught, abounding in it with thanksgiving." (vv. 6 & 7)

Note the amount of action words in the very first verse: walk, rooted, built, and established. There is clearly a call to action that goes way beyond the reception of our salvation. In fact, the call to action actually insinuates that "just as you received Jesus, *SO YOU ALSO SHOULD...*" Meaning, this should be the continuum of your salvation... a non-negotiable, automatic, default lifestyle that is like an "if-then" statement that has been programmed into a computer. But a call to action is simply an invitation, and an invitation requires a response. An invitation to a party doesn't mean I am experiencing the party. In order for the party to become my reality, I must respond and then attend. I must engage in an intentional act. Even if I RSVP and say I am coming, I still have to reserve that day on my calendar, prioritize it, prepare for it, and ultimately show up for it! My point is there is a part that we play in experiencing the "party" of the Spirit. We must engage in action and partner with God in the releasing of the "fullness of the Godhead bodily." That is the reward... to find our completion and our fulfillment in Him!

THE WARNING

> *"Beware lest anyone cheat you through philosophy and empty deceit, according to the tradition of men, according to the basic principles of the world, and not according to Christ." (v. 8)*

The "basic principles of the world" is your system. I think it is worthy to note that many Scripture versions say not to be "taken captive" by the principles of the world instead of using the word "cheat" in this verse. To be taken captive means to be enslaved, locked up, and "stuck." It is the idea of being (or feeling) trapped... like there is no way out! Whether it is the word *cheated* or the phrase *taken captive*, the warning is that you are being kept from something. In this case, you are being kept from your true design in Christ and ultimately from fulfilling your purpose. There is no completion in the world, and there certainly is no satisfaction. The demands of its principles are too hard to keep up with; again, a moving target that will keep you forever aiming, but always falling short of the bullseye.

THE REWARD

> *"For in Him dwells all the fullness of the Godhead bodily; and you are complete in Him, who is the head of all principality and power." (Col. 2:9&10 NKJV)*

Ah yes! The reward. The goal. The bullseye. Here we have the "then" part of the "if-then" statement. If you respond to the invitation to build yourself up in Jesus, if you continue in your journey of faith and press into your deeply rooted God-design, then you will come into and experience your completeness, your design. This is the fulfillment that we all long for—to go beyond just knowing who we are to actually live out who we are!

> *"As for me, I will see Your face in righteousness; I SHALL BE SATISFIED WHEN I WAKE IN YOUR LIKENESS." (Psalm 17:15 NKJV Emphasis mine)*

In Psalm 17, David wrestles with the ways and the wickedness of the world and the lies, deceptions, oppression, and oppositions he faces. He speaks of the temporary satisfaction brought about by worldly possessions. But he ends the whole psalm with this climatic declaration. He proclaims that his life is not about what he possesses, but about who he is becoming. David knows that satisfaction and completeness is achieved by living out the person of God in his life. The reward is coming into His likeness and experiencing the Godhead bodily.

It is important that you know that not experiencing this fullness does not negate the truth of it, nor does it mean that the Godhead bodily does not already reside in you. It simply means it has not yet become your reality. It is through your action that your God-design is activated! This is how we partner with God; it is the part that we get to play in releasing the fullness of the kingdom through our lives!

Read this whole passage from The Passion translation.

"In the same way you received Jesus our Lord and Messiah by faith, continue your journey of faith, progressing further into your union with him! Your spiritual roots go deeply into his life as you are continually infused with strength, encouraged in every way. For you are established in the faith you have absorbed and enriched by your devotion to him!

"Beware that no one distracts you or intimidates you in their attempt to lead you away from Christ's fullness by pretending to be full of wisdom when they're filled with endless arguments of human logic. For they operate with humanistic and clouded judgments based on the mindset of this world system, and not the anointed truths of the Anointed One.

"For he is the complete fullness of deity living in human form. And our own completeness is now found in him. We are completely filled with God as Christ's fullness overflows within us. He is the Head of every kingdom and authority in the universe!"

SYSTEM + EXPERIENCE

So how does this passage connect with our core beliefs? Simply said, our core beliefs have become the sum total of life's "inputs." Just like 2 + 2 = 4, our education + our parents = a belief. Or our culture + our church doctrine = a belief. That is how the influence of our system establishes the foundation upon which we grow and the roots from which we are fed. If you were raised up in an environment that knew Jesus and was built upon biblical foundations, then it's possible you are ahead of those of us who were not. However, the warning in Colossians reminds us that even those who are believers will wrestle with the voice of the world. In fact, this passage is written TO believers! This means that as believers, we are just as susceptible to the dangers of the voices of human logic, intellect, philosophy, clouded judgments, traditions of men, and the basic principles of the world. They are a threat to the "anointed truths of the Anointed One," meaning the reality of God's kingdom-principles. It's the mindset of the world and its ruthless ever-changing definitions that keep us stumbling and fumbling, starving for love and acceptance! It is a faulty foundation and there is no permanent security in it.

Let's take a moment to talk about the power of experience. Our life is also the sum total of our experiences. I often say, your system + your experience = your core beliefs. While God has designed us for experience, the enemy will use experience to lie to us and develop a faulty foundation. Patterns of thinking and feeling are not just molded by our system, but also by our experience IN the system, or HOW we experience our system. In other words, what we are feeling and thinking in the midst of an experience.

The word *experience* means "the process of getting knowledge or skill that is obtained from doing, seeing, or feeling things, or something that happens which has an effect on you." The verb form "to experience" means "to have something happen to you; to do or feel something." While we gain knowledge from experience, we also develop emotional and relational habits through experience. Think about how much your feelings about a current situation are predetermined by how you experienced it in the past. You may not even realize it, but they are! Our brain forms habitual ruts that become our "go to" emotion or thought in any given situation, and those ruts are formed through past experience. Ultimately, much like our system, core beliefs are established through this process. We will be attacking this in more detail, but for now, let it be said that our experiences highly impact what we feel and think in any given situation, which is a faulty (and fickle) foundation.

So, the reality is that our system + our experiences WITHOUT JESUS = FALSE core beliefs that are filled with lies and limitations. This too often is the faulty foundation that we build our lives on—even as believers! This is the warning given in the passage above.

But praise be to God, there is another foundation that has been given to us, and this foundation has a name, and that name is Jesus Christ. I pray that you see the difference between the two foundations. One is faulty, and the other is firm. One may be your reality, but the other is your truth. In other words, your reality does not always equal truth!

Jesus is to be your cornerstone; He IS the plumb line upon which you find the measurement to build life! You must respond to the invitation to build upon HIS truth, to establish your life upon His kingdom principles, to be fed and nourished with His Word, and to live it out! Remember, your action activates what is already accomplished in you. This is a crucial part of enforcing YOU. This is why the "Enforcing You" sections are included with every chapter. They are to teach you by demonstration how to actively begin to use the Word to plant your feet on the firm foundation of Him, His truths, and His design for you!

Prayer Practice:

Father I thank You that YOU are the perfect standard. In You, there is no shifting or changing, and I always find constancy; a firm foundation where my ankles will not turn. Who is like You, God, and what can this world offer? Only You bring me peace, safety, and security. Only You bring me confidence and courage! Who is like You? I praise You for placing my feet upon a rock—THE ROCK—and I stand with strong legs and arms lifted high. I believe You, God, in all things...I believe what you say, not what my system tells me or what my experiences have told me, or even what my feelings are screaming. My opinion is nothing. My life is a lie without Your presence and love. Hallelujah to the ONE TRUE VOICE...the voice of the God of creation, MY Creator, MY God, MY firm foundation! In Jesus' name, amen.

Enforcing You

Passage:

"Then Jesus said to those Jews who believed Him, 'If you abide in My Word, you are My disciples indeed. And you shall know the truth, and the truth shall make you free." (John 8:31&32 NKJV)

Declaration:

Father, I thank You that as I abide in Your Word, the revelation of what is true is revealed to me through Your Holy Spirit. I rejoice that Your truth breaks every lie off of me and shifts me into freedom. I choose Your Word as my truth and I receive the freedom that it brings. Your Word is my foundation of truth.

Self-reconciliation:

[Say your name], as you abide, remain, and tarry in the Word of God, the knowledge of truth is revealed to you. You are neither in the dark nor without direction. You have the light of His Word guiding every step. You are not trapped nor are you stuck by your circumstances, thoughts, emotions, or relationships. You are free! His truths have liberated your heart and your mind, and you are grounded upon His foundation of freedom.

Passage:

"If any of you lacks wisdom, let him ask of God, who gives to all liberally and without reproach, and it will be given to him." (James 1:5 NKJV)

Declaration:

I thank You, God, for the promise of Your wisdom that is given to me liberally. You give, not because of anything I have done, but because I ask for it and receive it. I recognize that my only source of true wisdom is found in You. I receive it to the fullest and receive the confidence it brings.

Self-reconciliation:

[Say your name], you have been given the wisdom of God liberally in Christ. He is generous with you and empowers you to walk in that wisdom. I speak a closing of your ears to the wisdom of the world and its voice and an opening of your ears to the wisdom of God and His voice. Because of His wisdom, you are secure and confident in all things!

Passage:

"Every good gift and every perfect gift is from above, and comes down from the Father of lights, with whom there is no variation of shadow of turning." (James 1:17 NKJV)

Declaration:

O how great it is to know that I serve a God who is consistent and constant. There is no variation with You. You are a stable, firm foundation that I can count on. I praise You that You do not shift like the world does, but that you remain the same yesterday, today, and forever.

Self-reconciliation:

[Say your name], God Himself is your Father and He provides you with a stable foundation where you can stand with confidence. You are safe and secure in the knowledge that He does not change. Though the world changes and your circumstances change, He remains the same. In that truth, you are at peace. Because He does not shift who He is in the midst of different circumstances, neither do you. Just as His character is constant, so you are constant. Your character is not a variable that shifts. It is rooted in the person of Jesus!

Passage:
"So the Lord, the Eternal, has this to say:

'Eternal One: See here, I am laying in Zion a stone, a tested stone—a cornerstone, chosen and precious—for a firm foundation.

'Whoever trusts in it will never be disgraced. Justice will be the line by which I lay out its floor plan, and righteousness will be My leveling tool. A hailstorm will pulverize and wash away the fraud and deception behind which people hide, and floodwaters will overrun their hiding place.'"
(Isaiah 28:16-17 The Voice)

Declaration:
What peace I have knowing that You have provided a firm foundation upon which I can stand with confidence. I choose to trust You and Your standard as the floor plan for my life. I thank You that You have designed me according to Your blueprints and I rejoice in knowing that You are my measuring tool for life. Every other standard is faulty, but you are tried and true...the one firm foundation that does not shake when the world does.

Self-reconciliaton:

[Say your name], Jesus is the only standard of measurement with any influence in your heart. Shift your eyes away from the fickleness of the world and onto Jesus, your firm foundation. You are at rest in the peace and ease that He has released in you. You are created in His design. His heart is your floor plan. Just as He is, so you are. You are settled in the rest of His standard and you are confident in what He says about you. He is the rock upon which you were designed and upon which you stand. Your feet are grounded in His heart and you will not be moved! In times of great storms, you remain anchored and are not tossed by the winds and waves around you.

————————

Passage:

"Stand fast therefore in the liberty by which Christ has made us free, and do not be entangled again with a yoke of bondage...

"You have become estranged from Christ, you who attempt to be justified by law; you have fallen from grace. For we through the Spirit eagerly wait for the hope of righteousness by faith. For in Christ Jesus neither circumcision nor uncircumcision avails anything, but faith working through love.

*"You ran well. Who hindered you from obeying the truth? **This persuasion does not come from Him who calls you.** A little leaven leavens the whole lump." (Galatians 5:1,4-9 NKJV)*

Declaration:

Thank You, God for freedom in Jesus and the grace to walk in that freedom. There are no chains on me! Thank You for opening my eyes to recognize where the world tries to captivate me and pull me away from You through its tireless demands. Because of Your Spirit, I am not estranged from You, for I have been persuaded by Your love and any other persuasion I reject... by faith I rest in Your liberty!

Self-reconciliation:

[Say your name], you are free... free from all that would entangle you and weigh you down. Any pressure that you feel that causes haste or angst is not from God and you know this well. You are not under the watch of the world. You are saturated in the liberating truth of Jesus. He is your persuasion. I break all other influence off of your mind and out of your heart...for you are free! The love of God persuades you in all things. Stand in your freedom and refuse to be enslaved to the urgencies and demands around you. Any chain that you experience is a thief and a liar and I take authority over them in the name of Jesus. He is the key that has set you free. Your heart and mind are skipping, running, and dancing through all of life and in every season because you function only in accordance to the Spirit... for where the Spirit of the Lord is, there is liberty!

Chapter Three
The Power of Core Beliefs

"For as he thinks in his heart, so is he."
(Proverbs 23:7 NKJV)

This is a common verse that many of us have heard quoted. You might even quote it yourself. What is God really saying to us in this verse? Too often we nod our heads at commonly quoted verses, and we think we know what is being said or what is meant, but *do we really*? Let's dive into these words and discover what God is saying regarding enforcing YOU, and how this verse captures the power that our thoughts and emotions have to navigate who we become.

The word *heart* in this verse comes from the Hebrew word "nephesh" which is translated into the English word "soul" 475 times in the Bible. The definition includes "soul, self, appetite, mind, desire, emotion, passion; activity of mind, will and character." Hence the phrase, "as the heart thinks," which includes both the heart and the mind. This verse is not referring to your spiritual being; it is referring to your soul, or your personality (what you think, feel, and ultimately choose). So what does this mean? This means that what we believe in our minds, feel in our hearts, and the choices that we make actually form or design who we become. This is great news! This means that we don't have to be victims, but we have been empowered to choose who we want to be. This starts in the heart and mind... the core of your beliefs. Your core beliefs are the foundation upon which you navigate, or build, your life. To reiterate the idea from chapter 2, this is why it is so important that you are rooted and built up in Christ.

Whether you realize it or not, your core beliefs are navigating your life. They don't just navigate the choices you make, but they also navigate how you feel and what you think about any given situation. Moreover, core beliefs actually have the power to determine how you will receive or perceive any situation.

Let me try to simplify this concept in one statement:

> "Your core beliefs predetermine how you perceive, what your perspective is, and ultimately what your paradigm (your reality) will become."

If I were preaching, I would say it again, but since you are reading...let me write it for you to read one more time:

> "Your core beliefs predetermine how you perceive, what your perspective is, and ultimately what your paradigm (your

reality) will become."

I mentioned in the introduction that when writing "This is Me," the Lord gave me a revelation that changed my life and showed me how to enforce my design. This was it! This single statement is what inspired this book, and if you remember nothing else, I hope you get this concept.

Before I break this statement down, let me give you a real-life example of how this works.

If I have always believed in my heart (a core belief) that I am unloved, or not worthy of being loved, then no matter how much people around me try to show or express love, I will likely still perceive a lack of love. My perception of how I feel will then become my perspective (what I see) when I am around those people. My perspective is my operating truth. This perception and perspective of course then affect my behavior, which develops into patterns of behaving... and ultimately becomes the paradigm or reality of my life. It is a self-fulfilling prophecy!

What I believe in my heart (my belief system, sometimes referred to as "BS" – pun intended) actually navigates the reality I live in. And remember, my reality does not always equal what is true. Usually, we are living according to the "BS" that has been developed by our systems and experiences.

Think about it, we all know someone who always feels rejected no matter how hard we try to make them feel accepted. Over time, those people become difficult to love... they are frustrating and can be very challenging to be around (especially if you also struggle with feeling rejected). You see how this cycle works? It is a trick of the devil that keeps us starving and unsatisfied.

We teach and train people how to treat us by the way we treat ourselves in our own minds. Simply said, the way you feel about who you are is one of the biggest factors in how people will treat you! Someone who thinks they are weak sends the message, "I need help," which then teaches people around them to always do everything for them, which sends the message, "you are weak." Not only does it teach those around them, but also their core belief (lie) actually becomes their reality, which they then equate with truth...even though it is based on "BS." In this case, "weakness" becomes the paradigm of their life. I see this in unhealthy relationships all the time. There may be a dominant, or even abusive, partner, but we find that even the less dominant, or victim, plays a part in the development of that pattern. I go into great depths on this in my book *To Love and To Be Loved*. We play a part in the personality of any relationship... the way people treat us is primarily developed by the way we treat ourselves. This starts in your own heart. What do you believe about you? This is why we see patterns of relationships. Until we change the way we see ourselves, we won't change our paradigm.

PERCEPTION

In my book *To Love and To Be Loved*, I write about a Ted Talk called "The Art of Being Yourself." In short, the speaker talked about how all of life is basically all about discovering who we really are. In other words, believer or not, we all wrestle with the question, "Who am I?" The speaker goes on to talk about the multiple perceptions that we wrestle with in life. As believers we are not exempt from this battle.

We battle with the perception of man (who people say that we are, their interpretation), our perception of self (who we say we are, our own interpretation), and of course there is the perception of God (who God says we are, His interpretation).

Paul reconciles these perceptions in Corinthians when he realizes that the world is filled with judgment... that of those around him, the judgment that is within him, and the judgment of God.

> *"But with me it is a very small thing that I should be judged by you or by a human court. In fact, I do not even judge myself. For I know of nothing against myself, yet I am not justified by this; but He who judges me is the Lord." (1 Corinthians 4:3 NKJV)*

Isn't it true that we struggle with these same perceptions? Battling to decide what we will choose to believe in any given moment? This is the problem with the faulty foundation... it is unstable and unsettling. It simply does not provide the confidence that we need in a moment to perceive accurately.

Instead, a faulty foundation leaves us perceiving through our experiences (my opinions and feelings) and our system (the opinions and feelings of others). But where is God in that? Paul recognizes that the only accurate perception is founded in seeking God's opinion on the matter. Not, "What does man think?" Not, "What do I think?" Not, "What have my experiences told me?" But, "What does God think?"

Let's take a look at what the word *perception* actually means. By definition, perception means "the ability to see, hear, or become aware of something through the senses; an awareness of something through the senses; the neurophysiological processes, including memory, by which an organism becomes aware of and interprets external stimuli."

The important thing for you to understand is that perception involves the senses. It is what you interpret or what you conclude through your senses. This includes how you feel. This means that perception is not necessarily factual, but rather how we interpret the facts based on our senses, or how we are personally experiencing that moment. It is your understanding of a given situation, person or object filtered through all your senses.

When understanding perception, it is also important to recognize how experience comes in to play here. A situation that resembles something we've previously experienced will typically connect us immediately to the emotions we had in that previous situation as well. It is like déjà vu, which is "the feeling of having already experienced the present situation." Again, it is highly sensual and will affect my perception in that moment. The problem is sometimes we don't realize that our previous experience can be jading the reality of current experience because it is being viewed and experienced emotionally.

It is possible for you and me to be in the same situation or maybe hear the same conversation but perceive it completely differently. I see this frequently when I am working with couples in counseling. They can literally sit in the same room and share the same story and factually be in agreement. Yet, they both have totally different perceptions. Why? Because how they see in that moment is highly influenced by what they already believe in their own minds and hearts and how they have previously experienced moments like that one. Neither one is wrong, but they both perceive differently. This is why our core beliefs about who we are and what we believe predetermine how we will perceive. Perception is how you see in a moment.

PERSPECTIVE

Your perception becomes the lens you see through that ultimately determines what you see. In other words, how I see (my perception) determines my perspective (what I see). Perspective means "a particular attitude toward or way of regarding something; a point of view." In short, perspective is how I interpret what I see, it is what I conclude as my point of view. Think about it, you and I can be watching the same circumstance that is taking place in the middle of the room. Let's say it is an argument between two people. I am standing in one corner and you are standing in the opposite corner. I see one person's face, but you see the other. Although we are standing in the same room, watching the same fight, we will no doubt have different perspectives because we literally have different vantage points. Our personal perceptions (how we each feel) often position us in those two different corners, which give us each our own points of view. Listen, this is important, because when we can wrap our brains around this concept, we will understand why two people can argue, yet both seem to be right. And both in some way *are* right, when we see it from each one's perspective. This requires first seeking to understand the other's side, heart, past system, and experiences.

This is what's referred to in Proverbs 18:17:

"The first one to plead his cause seems right,
Until his neighbor comes and examines him."

This proverb is referring to the fact that only hearing "one side of the story" always seems right, until you examine the heart and motive of the person telling the story. This is the whole purpose of "cross examination" in a trial. It is important to note that when someone is cross-examined, the lawyer is not necessarily trying to prove that the person on the stand is lying, the lawyer is trying to expose where understanding or perspective is faulty. This is typically brought to light by exposing a bias or core belief that would predetermine or incorrectly navigate the person to a tainted perspective. Facts that are left out, assumptions that are made, feelings that are involved... these are all things that are used to cross-examine someone. Too often we assume one person in a conflict must be lying, but that is not always the case! However, if all we ever heard was one side of a story, then that one person would always be right because we have not taken the time to fully examine that heart of each side.

Therefore, it is important to understand the other person before you seek to be understood. In most arguments, our goal is to get the other person to see things from our point of view. Moreover, we want them to agree with our point of view. The problem is our point of view is often filtered through our skewed perception of our system and experiences. This means we see from a "faulty angle" because we are grounded on a faulty foundation. If we learn this about ourselves, we will recognize it in others, and it will change the way we respond to them. But this requires me to have the perspective of Christ. Good news! As believers we have been given that perspective!

"But God, who is rich in mercy, because of His great love with which He loved us, even when we were dead in trespasses, made us alive together with Christ (by grace you have been

saved), and raised us up together, and made us
sit together in the heavenly places in Christ
Jesus." (Eph. 2:4&5 NKJV)

Spiritually, we have been positioned in the "heavenly places," which gives us a whole new point of view. We don't have to see things horizontally; we get to look down and see things from the Father's view. His perspective becomes your perspective. This is what Paul was talking about in 1 Corinthians 4:3 (above) when he said he settles in the judgment of God, meaning, he agrees with God's perspective. More specifically, he agrees with God in the way God sees him! So, in any given moment, if we are not seeing from God's perspective, our point of view will be tainted and from a faulty, worldly, "system and experience-influenced" angle.

Being rooted in and fixed on Christ establishes core beliefs that cause us to see things the way He does. Most importantly, it causes us to see ourselves His way. Meaning, when I look into the mirror, I see what He sees, and I see it the way He sees it! This is what we are doing when we are self-reconciling; we are stating to ourselves that we agree with God regarding who we are.

> *"So from now on we regard no one from a*
> *worldly point of view..."*
> *(2 Corinthians 5:16 NKJV)*

We must see this verse as relevant to how we

regard ourselves as well as others. When God sees us, He doesn't see our flesh, He sees the beauty of His design within us, the new creation in Christ! Verse 17 of 2 Corinthians 5 reads:

> "Therefore, if anyone is in Christ, he IS a new creation; old things have passed away; behold, all things have become new."

This verse clearly tells me that I am a new creation right now! All my old patterns, old behaviors, old beliefs, old fears, old habits are done away with...God doesn't see those things when He looks at me. Unfortunately, the enemy, the world, and our flesh will conspire together to keep me from seeing myself that way.

The word "behold" in the original language denotes the idea of "seeing or to perceive with the eyes." It also includes the idea of "cherishing and paying attention to (something)." I think it is possible that if we want to see what God sees, we must choose to see it, perceive it, and then cherish and pay attention to it. This is why I think talking self-reconciliation habits into a mirror are so important... you must be intentional to see and pay attention to yourself!

God looks at us according to our spirit and treats us according to our "God-potential." His perspective only sees His definition, not the world's. Unfortunately, we too often don't see that in ourselves. We only see our faults and shortcomings, and they are typically established from the world's perspective. If only we would cherish what He sees when we look into the mirror!!

PARADIGM

So how does this all lead to the way we live our lives? Let's go back to the verse at the beginning of this chapter.

> *"For as he thinks in his heart, so is he."*
> *(Proverbs 23:7)*

This verse clearly reminds us that who we become is formed by what it is in our hearts. Remember, the word *heart* here means activity of mind, will (desire), and character. I think it is fair to say that what you believe, you will become. Hence, your core beliefs ultimately mold your paradigm.

Paradigm refers to a pattern, a model, or a mold. In this case, we are referring to the pattern by which you live, or the mold your life "fits into." The important thing to note is that your core beliefs are the mold by which patterns are developed and paradigms are established.

Think about a cake pan and how the batter takes on the shape of the pan. Whatever cake design I want to make, I can do it, I just need to the right mold to pour the batter into. This is the case with our core beliefs. If I use the mold of the world, then I will take on the form of the world; the way the world thinks, feels, and reasons... its logic, philosophy and traditions. (Refer back to Colossians 2:8) But remember, God says, "as He is, so are we in this world..." (1 John 4:17) He is your mold! You are created in His design. However, I must choose to pour my life continually into Him if I want that mold be the shape of my life. As I pour into Him, my paradigm will take the shape of kingdom-principles and heavenly characteristics.

> *"Your kingdom come. Your will be done on earth as it is in heaven."*
> *(Matthew 6:10 NKJV)*

Our lives are to be the demonstration of the Kingdom of Heaven here on Earth. We are the intersection where Heaven meets Earth. Moreover, our stories are to be the presentation of Heaven's possibilities to those around us and our design is to reflect the person of Jesus. Jesus came to the earth and pinned the kingdom here (the third heavens to the first heavens), and we are the pin that holds it here! The mold for living free here on Earth is available in Christ. As we align our souls with His person ("work out our salvation" and "train ourselves towards righteousness" Phil. 2:13 and 1 Tim. 4:7), our personalities and our paradigms will take on His form. (Proverbs 23:7) But, make no mistake, even if you choose not to take on His form, it is indeed established!

As a counselor, I can often point out the root heart issue in an individual just by looking at the pattern of his or her life. The "shape" or "form" of their behaviors will look like the mold of their beliefs. If I live in the mold (or belief) of fear, then every experience, situation, conversation, etc. will be shaped by fear and filtered through fear. My perception will be tainted by fear and my perspective will see fear... and I will conclude fear and respond accordingly... In fear! Because "your core beliefs predetermine how you perceive, what your perspective is and ultimately what your paradigm (your reality) will become."

One might tell me about a life of rejection, and I can very easily conclude that this person sees himself or herself as unworthy, not acceptable, not good enough or unlovable. At this point, we could stop and discuss which came first, the experience or the belief, but where or how it started isn't the point. The good news is that it can be changed! By changing your core belief, you can change your paradigm. This is done by rooting yourself in Christ and seeing *how* He sees (His perception) and seeing *what* He sees (His perspective).

Please note that choosing Christ's perspective does not mean you will no longer experience rejection in this world. Everyone experiences rejection. What it does mean is that you don't have to allow rejection to be the thing that defines you. You don't have to allow rejection to mold your beliefs about who you are. Your truth comes from somewhere else. Coming into this understanding ultimately will change the way you act, respond, behave, choose, relate, love, and receive love... and that will cause a shift in your paradigm!

Starting in the heart and mind is often the opposite of the pattern we settle into. Typically, we think that we change our mind by changing our circumstances (our paradigm). In other words, we wait on our circumstances to change before we choose to be rooted in joy, or love, or grace, or hope, or kindness, or peace, or... fill in the blank. But the Bible reminds us in Mark 16:17 that His followers are to function on faith, and signs will follow.

Let's be honest, sometimes we wait to operate in the character of Christ until we see or experience what we want. That simply is not faith... faith is operating in love, even when you don't feel or see love. Faith is forgiving someone when they haven't sought it. Faith is responding in gentleness to anger. I think we forget what it means to feel things on faith, or think things on faith, or believe things on faith, specifically regarding how we feel, think, or believe about ourselves. I believe this is part of what Jesus referred to when He exhorted the Pharisees to first clean the inside of the cup (Matthew 23:26, Luke 11:39). Or what Paul was saying in Romans 4:16 when he said, "the promise should be sure of the seed," and "gives life to the dead and calls those things which do not exist as though they did..." It's the idea of being so confident in what has been spoken, your God-design, that you act like it even when you don't feel like it! I tell my clients this is what it means to "faith it until you become it." If the

Word says it, then you can believe it, even if you don't see it!

We will delve more into how to change our core beliefs in the next chapter, but for now, let it be said that you are not stuck or victimized by your paradigm. You can change the pattern of your life, but it starts on the inside of YOU!

So let's review:

> "Your core beliefs predetermine how you perceive, what your perspective is, and ultimately what your paradigm (your reality) will become."

This whole book is written to help you enforce God's core beliefs about YOU into your life. Ultimately that is how you enforce YOU! That is why it is so important that you practice the Enforcing YOU portions. It is only by His truths that your heart is yanked into alignment with His, and your core beliefs are made synonymous with what He says. The Word is your blueprint that exposes where your soul is not in likeness with what He says. That is what we are told in Hebrews 4:12:

> *"For the word of God is living and powerful, and sharper than any two-edged sword, piercing even to the division of soul and spirit, and of joints and marrow, and is a discerner of the thoughts and intents of the*

heart."

The Word of God exposes and reveals where our hearts are rooted. It causes us to see any division between the soul and the spirit. I like to say it is like being filleted like a fish, laid open, and then gutted of any "parts" that are not nutritious or healthy... His Word is the knife that slices you open to look inside... beyond the paradigm and into the core of your being. This is the first step in enforcing YOU. You must start with your core beliefs!

Prayer Practice:
Father, thank You for the truth that as I change what I believe in my heart, my mind will change, the way I see things will be aligned with You, and ultimately, my life will change. Thank You that I am not a victim. You have given me the authority to take captive every thought and drag it into alignment with Your truth. Thank You that in every moment, there is a kingdom-perception and a kingdom-perspective. I close my eyes to the world's perspective, and I open my eyes to Your heavenly perspective. May I see from above and not from side to side, and may I respond with confidence, in the form of Your character and heart to all things at all times. In Jesus' name, amen!

Enforcing You

Passage:

"So from now on we regard no one from a worldly point of view..."
(2 Corinthians 5:16 NKJV)

Declaration:

Father, thank You for giving me Your heart and that in me is the full capacity to not see according to the flesh, but according to the Spirit. I receive the truth that I don't have to be reactive to flesh, but I get to respond to others in accordance to who they are created to be in Christ. Open my eyes that I would see from Your perspective and discern flesh from Spirit!

Self-reconciliation:

[Say your name], you are seated with Christ and have the same heavenly view as He has. Therefore, you don't see as the world sees and you pay no regard to what the world says. By the power and revelation of the Holy Spirit, you recognize the difference between your flesh and your Spirit, and you respond and walk in accordance to the Spirit in all things. Your flesh has no power, no say-so, and gets no opinion about things around you, or about YOU!

Passage:

"Therefore, if anyone is in Christ, he is a new creation; old things have passed away; behold, all things have become new." (2 Cor. 5:17)

Declaration:

What a glorious God You are and what a beautiful creation You have put in me! Thank You that You do all things well and completely! I agree with You that the old me has passed away and the new me is here, NOW! I rebuke any old patterns, habits, thoughts, feelings, or ways. I speak death over them and life into my new creation.

Self-reconciliation:

[Say your name], you are completely new in Christ! There is no amount of work that is needed; the blood of Jesus has established it. Your old man does not control you. Instead, you are surrendered to what already exists in you, which is the newness of Jesus. By the Spirit, your spiritual eyes see your new creation and your mind perceives it. Look deeply into who you are in Christ and pay attention to your new creation, cherish the beauty and nurture it!

Passage:

"But the fruit of the Spirit is love, joy, peace, forbearance, kindness, goodness, faithfulness, gentleness and self-control. Against such things there is no law. Those who belong to Christ Jesus have crucified the flesh with its passions and desires. Since we live by the Spirit, let us keep in step with the Spirit."

(Galatians 5:22-25 NKJV)

Declaration:

Father, thank You for empowering me with the fullness of the fruit of the Spirit. Thank You for putting evidence of Your character in me. I rejoice with You in the truth that my flesh is crucified along with temptation and sinful desires. You keep me in step with Your Spirit. Thank You that Your likeness dwells in entirety within me, and I submit myself completely to Your Spirit that my life may bloom the fruit of Your Spirit in abundance!

Self-reconciliation:

[Say your name], you are empowered with love, joy, peace, patience, kindness, goodness, faithfulness, gentleness, and self-control via the Holy Spirit. You bear this fruit simply by surrendering to God. It does not come by work nor by merit, but by grace it is the gift of God. Your flesh no longer has any life. It is dead. Your sinful passions, desires, and tendencies

have no hold on you—they were crucified with Jesus. As you surrender daily, you are in step with what you know is right—God's definition of the real you. You reap the fullness of who you are designed to be and are the display of His character to those around you!

Passage:

"But with me it is a very small thing that I should be judged by you or by a human court. In fact, I do not even judge myself. For I know of nothing against myself, yet I am not justified by this; but He who judges me is the Lord."
(1 Corinthians 4:3 NKJV)

Declaration:

What a relief to know, God, that You alone are my accountability. I do not have to receive the judgment of the world, nor do I need to judge myself. I have been justified completely by the blood of Jesus Christ!

Self-reconciliation:

[Say your name], you are free from the perceptions of the world! Its judgment has no hold and bears no weight. Your value and worth are not susceptible to opinions or evaluations! You no longer feel the need to assess yourself because you know the assessment of the Lord. It is done. You are confident that when He searches you, He reveals the beauty that is in you and reminds you of who you are and where you are

going. There is no human that can justify you, only Jesus can. And He did! Therefore, it is established!

Passage:

"Since, then, you have been raised with Christ, set your hearts on things above, where Christ is, seated at the right hand of God. Set your minds on things above, not on earthly things." (Colossians 3:1&2 NIV)

Declaration:

Thank You, Father, for raising me up with Christ. Thank You that a new life has been resurrected in Christ and that You positioned me with Jesus at Your right hand, and I have the benefits of a child. I set my mind upon You... I shift my thoughts from this world and intentionally place them on heaven... seeing from heaven's perspective and not giving in to the ways of the world!

Self-reconciliation:

[Say your name], you are not of this world. You are seated next to the right hand of the Father with Christ. You continually remember your kingdom benefits—His inheritance and His blessings that are within you. You do not have the mind nor perspectives of this world, but you see things from the Father's angle. You have the mind of Christ, and you don't think like the world. You are not distracted but are wholly devoted to kingdom principles and the ways of heaven!

Chapter Four
Reversing the Cycle

Read this statement again:

> "Your core beliefs predetermine how you perceive, what your perspective is, and ultimately what your paradigm (your reality) will become."

Being rooted in strong beliefs navigates our lives, but let's be honest, more often than not, our lives ultimately navigate what we believe. Moreover, instead of having an impact on the paradigm of the world, we too often allow the paradigm of the world to impact us. We are infiltrated with the world's opinions and if we are not rooted in Christ, we will be pulled into the world's way of thinking. Politics, education, religion, Hollywood... your entire system is telling you what to believe. You must open your eyes to see that you usurp your kingdom authority to impact the paradigm of the world when you give in to the beliefs of the world! We are called to be world-changers and to have dominion on the earth, not to lead defeated, victimized lives.

The problem isn't the church; the problem is within you and me. It is in our hearts and minds. Changing the world starts by making changes in you.

If you waver in what you believe about who you are, or you are not able to look at yourself and agree with what God says about you, how can you help others believe it? If you are not convinced, then how will you ever convince those around you? It is one thing to know who you are, it is another to be confident in it.

> "...being confident of this very thing, that He who has begun a good work in you will complete it until the day of Jesus Christ." (Phil. 1:6 NKJV)

To the same degree that we are confident in our salvation, we must be confident in who we are. God started it, and He will complete it! He is not a God who does things halfway, He is 100% in all His ways. Are you confident in this? Are you confident in your authority here on Earth... that you are an overcomer of the world because "greater is He who is in you than he who is in the world?" (1 John 4:4 NKJV).

THE CYCLE

The statement written at the beginning of this chapter is not a one-time thought. It is a cycle that keeps looping. From core beliefs, to perception, to perspective to paradigm—which then supports our core beliefs—and so on and so on. The cycle perpetuates as it feeds itself over and over. This is a GREAT concept when the cycle starts with the foundation of God's paradigm! Then you truly are grounded and rooted in Christ. The paradigm and pattern of the kingdom impresses on what you believe, as opposed to the patterns of the world impacting what you believe. His definition over the world's definition is the mold you form your image to. But again, I fear that too often we allow the paradigm of the world to impress our core beliefs and then we get stuck in that cycle. Our lives end up patterned according to false and faulty beliefs.

A PARADIGM SHIFT

Reversing this cycle is what we would call "a paradigm shift." A paradigm shift is "an important change that happens when the usual way of thinking about or doing something is replaced by a new and different way." What we need to do is train ourselves how to reverse the cycle... we need to replace our usual thought process with a new thought process. More specifically, we need to pattern our minds after God's thoughts!

> *"And do not be conformed to this world, but be transformed by the renewing of your mind, that you may prove what is that good and acceptable and perfect will of God."*
> *(Romans 12:2 NKJV)*

The word conform means "comply with rules, standards or laws, to behave according to socially acceptable standards, to be similar in form or type." This is exactly what we have been discussing; that the world has a standard that molds us into its "form," gives us social "rules," and allures us into behaving according to its social standards. Even more interesting is to note that the original Greek word used means "to fashion one's self (mind and character) to another's pattern." It denotes the idea of the essence of character and internal fashioning, as opposed to outer form or outline. In other words, the word conform, as used in this verse, refers to a molding of your identity.

The NIV version of this verse reads, "Do not be conformed *to the pattern* of the world (my emphasis), meaning the *blueprint* or *mold* of the world. But I would also like to present the idea that a pattern is developed only after we repeat a behavior over and over. In other words, a pattern is made from habits (a repeated behavior). Now there is a lot of brain science that we could go into around the idea of habits, but let it be said that habits actually develop paths in the brain called neural pathways. Once a neural pathway is developed, the behavior that developed that pathway becomes automatic and effortless.

Think about driving your car. Remember when you were first learning to drive how you had to be intentional to think about the steps that needed to be taken when starting the car? First put your foot on the brake, then turn the key, then move your foot off the brake, etc. It took a lot of intentional thinking and effort. You had to give your attention completely to the process. But now? Effortless! Why? Because the repeated behavior has turned into a habit and is simply just another pattern that has been developed in your life.

Like driving, other habitual behaviors create patterns that we fall into, without even thinking about them. Habitual thinking, habitual feelings, habitual responding—all create patterns in our lives. So not only has the world created a pattern, but in our attempts to appease the world, we have also developed patterns. Most are what I call survival patterns. You have probably heard them called coping mechanisms or coping skills. The problem is that when we address habits and patterns, we typically only focus on the behavior itself instead of focusing on the belief system BEHIND the behavior!

Here's the deal, when you decide to change your patterns, it will require effort... intentional focus and paying attention to the process. Remember, this is what it means to "behold." This is also what it means to "renew the mind."

Romans 12:2 doesn't just say "Don't be conformed..." it goes on to say, "be transformed!" How? By renewing your mind. Note the verb in this phrase, it is an action verb. You do the action. When we come into the knowledge of Jesus as our personal Savior, we are given a new mind. More specifically, we are given the mind of Christ (1 Cor. 2:16). However, our mind is in the habit of responding to our system and experiences, so we must renew our thoughts and create new neural pathways by practicing new thought patterns. This is the whole purpose of the

Enforcing YOU sections at the end of each chapter. It is one thing for me to teach or explain a concept, it is another to demonstrate it, and for you to engage in practicing the concept.

The word *transform* in Romans 12:2 comes from the Greek word "metamorphoo" which means "to change into another form, to transform, or transfigure." This Greek word is where we get the word metamorphosis, which refers to the transformational process an insect or amphibian goes through as it matures into an adult form. Biologically this physical transformation forces a change in behavior and environment. Consider a caterpillar that has gone through the transformation process of becoming a butterfly (metamorphosis). This caterpillar no longer has the same form or shape, and it also has completely different behaviors and is found in completely new environments. If we saw a butterfly crawling and never flying, grounded and never soaring, we would say that butterfly wasn't living to its fullest potential. We would see that instead of renewing its way of living according to its transformation, it has remained stuck and conformed to the pattern of the caterpillar. The butterfly has not beheld its new creation! I don't know about you, but if I saw a butterfly stuck in caterpillar behaviors, I would want to scream, "Don't you know what you have become? Don't you understand your potential? Do you not see how beautiful your new creation is?"

I think you know where I am going with this. Too many of us have been transformed into the image of Jesus. We have been brought into His likeness and have been given HIS personality. Yet we still take on the form of our old likeness and crawl when the Holy Spirit has given us wings to soar. We think the way we thought when we were broken and lost. We react out of wounds instead of responding out of healing. We behave like victims instead of victors, and we cower in fear instead of standing in boldness. We must understand that our salvation came with a transformation that is established whether we conform to our new creation or not. Just because the butterfly might choose not to fly does not negate that fact that it has wings and can fly. Conversely, our behavior does not negate our God-design and our potential. We must renew our minds from the perspective that it is already done!

Read this verse one more time from The Passion translation:

> *"Stop imitating the ideals and opinions of the culture around you, but be inwardly transformed by the Holy Spirit through a total reformation of how you think. This will empower you to discern God's will as you live a beautiful life, satisfying and perfect in his eyes."* *(Romans 12:2)*

THE WOMAN AT THE WELL

Let's take a look at an example of this concept in the Bible. In John 4, we encounter the longest conversation recorded in Scripture, and it takes place between Jesus and a woman. We know the story as "The Woman at the Well," but the story is about so much more. It reveals a lot about how encountering truth can change core beliefs, shatter lies, and shift your paradigm.

The story starts with a woman from Samaria who is going to a well in Sychar to draw water at high noon. While she is there, Jesus "just happens to be" sitting next to the well. (Interesting side note, the Bible says that Jesus "must needed go" to Sychar... meaning the Spirit allured Him and positioned Him... for such a time as this!) There is significance to the timing of the encounter. Because of the heat during the day, morning and dusk were the times that people would draw water. This means at noon it would be more likely that no one would be there. Now, Scripture doesn't say, but I think it is fair to assume, as we learn more about this woman's system and experiences, that she was avoiding people. In my book *To Love and To Be Loved,* I go into great detail about how connection requires vulnerability and feeling emotionally safe. That said, through the conversation between the woman and Jesus, we learn that she has had five husbands in the past, moreover, the man she was currently living with was not her husband. Before we go any further, here is an important cultural fact (rule of the system) that will help you gain insight into this woman's experience: only men had the power to marry and divorce in their culture. This means that this woman had experienced rejection and/or loss five times and was currently in a situation where a man was willing to live with her, but not marry her. I would like to propose to you that although this woman was likely seen and labeled as an adulteress, she was also a very rejected and unloved woman. Her system called her "adulteress," and her experience called her "rejected." This equaled a reality of judgment, isolation, shame, lack of love, disconnection, and rejection. This was her foundation; her roots that established a core belief that she really was unworthy. This was, no doubt, a core lie in her heart and mind!

Are you seeing how she demonstrates the concept: "Your core beliefs predetermine how you perceive, what your perspective is, and ultimately what your paradigm (your reality) will become"? The fact that this woman did not feel "safe" to connect with people tells us that she operated in fear of rejection and "unlovability." Because of her system and her experience, I think it is fair to assume that she believed that she was not lovable and not worthy of connection... and that her life was considered unacceptable. This core belief (core lie) ultimately decided the paradigm of her life, which in this case was her pattern of broken relationships and going to the well alone and disconnected. That paradigm confirmed her core beliefs that she was unworthy and rejected... worthy of loneliness and isolation. That's how the cycle spins. Furthermore, I am confident that her core lie of rejection predetermined how she perceived every interaction, what she concluded in her relationships as well as her perspective of herself.

Note that in verse 9 of John 4 she says, "Why would a Jewish man ask a Samaritan woman for a drink of water?" The woman clearly thought like her system and could not understand why Jesus was talking to her—"a Samaritan woman." She took on the identity of her culture that defined the paradigm of what was and was not appropriate. Not only that, but her core belief was subtly trying to pull Jesus into that paradigm as well. Remember, what we believe about who we are will teach and train others how to treat us. Jesus shattered the paradigm of her system and presented to her a new paradigm that came with a new system with kingdom mentality; new core beliefs with a new way of perceiving, a new perspective and ultimately a new way of life. He offered her a paradigm shift.

Let's zoom in and see what happens when the woman encounters truth and how her cycle gets reversed. Jesus presents to her a truth that trumps her reality. He does not ignore her reality; He presents her with a truth that overshadows it! She is being presented with the opportunity to be transformed by unconditional love and acceptance. This is a whole new message for her. He offers, and she has to choose to receive it! Once she recognizes the love He offers, AND SHE BELIEVES IT AND RECEIVES IT, the shift begins. The foundation on which she was established, and the traditions and opinions of man were officially shaken and cracked. The woman had to do more than just have knowledge of truth, she had to personalize it. She had to receive it for herself and make it true for her. This was her moment of truth. She now had two messages to wrestle with and she needed to make a decision. "Which one will I believe, FOR ME?"

We learn her answer in the next scene of John 4. The woman went back to Samaria and told the whole town: "Come, see a Man who told me all things that I ever did." For her to do this would have definitely required a miraculous mindset change, both in her confidence and her understanding of who she was. This woman clearly had an identity shift that caused a paradigm shift. No longer hiding and isolating herself, no longer settling in rejection, shame, and embarrassment, she was ready to face the entire town (including the men). Not only did she stand, openly seen, she addressed "the elephant" of her past. This paradigm shift started in her core beliefs about herself.

Every day we are faced with multiple messages, voices that try to define what is or is not true for each of us. That's reality. Walking in your identity doesn't mean you will never wrestle with false truths or battle with negative thoughts and emotions. What it does mean is you CHOOSE to settle on what God says is true about you. This isn't always how you feel, or think, or what your reality says, but it is what you must choose to believe and stand on. This is why we live by faith, not by sight, feelings, or thoughts.

In the next chapter, I am going to go into more

detail on how to practice renewing your mind in order to shift your paradigm and start enforcing YOU.

Prayer Practice:

God, thank You for shifting the paradigm of my life; Your paradigm is true. I rejoice in the message You speak over my life and I believe and receive Your love as my truth. I stand in Your love, firm and confident in my position as Your daughter, and I release the posture of Jesus in all I think, feel, and do. Thank You for simplifying my life and for having a heavenly paradigm that I have been brought into. In Jesus' name, amen.

Enforcing You

Passage:

"...being confident of this very thing, that He who has begun a good work in you will complete it until the day of Jesus Christ." (Phil. 1:6 NKJV)

Declaration:

God, You are a God who completes everything, and You complete it with excellence. You are ever working towards completion and You never give up or walk away with things half done. Thank You that I can be confident that I will never be left abandoned, but that just as You initiated every good work in my life, You are faithful to complete it!

Self-reconciliation:

[Say your name], confidence is in you, and you are confident that God is working in your life. There is not fear or doubt that looms in your mind or heart. You stand in boldness knowing that God is completing you. There is no strife and work in your flesh, but rather you sit in peace because you are confident that He who has begun the work in you will complete it until the day of Christ Jesus.

Passage:

"Yet in all these things we are more than conquerors through Him who loved us." (Romans 8:37 NKJV)

Declaration:

I stand in agreement with You, God, and declare that I am more than a conqueror in Christ and that Your love leads me in victory. I declare that because of Your love, no thought outside of Your love can overtake me. This is my truth today and tomorrow and forever more. You have established my victory!

Self-reconciliation:

[Say your name], you are not just a conqueror. Through Christ, you are more than a conqueror. You are established in your victory, and you live from the side of victory, therefore, there is no defeat, you are not a victim, and you are not an underdog in Christ. Walk with a victorious step in all you do and manifest what you know to be true in your spirit!

Passage:

"For 'who has known the mind of the Lord that he may instruct Him?' But we have the mind of Christ." (1 Cor. 2:16 NKJV)

"For 'who has ever intimately known the mind of the Lord Yahweh well enough to become his counselor?' Christ has, and we possess Christ perceptions." (1 Cor. 2:16 The Passion Translation)

Declaration:

Father, I praise You for giving me the mind of Christ and with it the ability to see, think, feel, and perceive like You! I declare that I have the mind of Christ and just as You think, I think; and just as You perceive, I perceive. I declare that I am free from the perceptions of the world and have been brought into the perceptions of the kingdom.

Self-reconciliation:

[Say your name], you have the mind of Christ and have been set free from the thoughts of the world. You no longer think the way you used to. Your way of thinking and perceiving has been reversed. You have shifted in your understanding and changed your paradigm because you think according to Christ and not your intellect or emotions; you think according to the kingdom and not the world; you think according to your promises and not your experiences. Today, your paradigm will manifest your kingdom truths.

Passage:

"Now the Lord is the Spirit; and where the Spirit of the Lord is, there is liberty" (2 Cor. 3:17 NKJV)

Declaration:

I declare that I am free because of the Spirit of God living and breathing within me. I rejoice in the liberty that is in my life and I receive the fullness of

Your freedom. Thank You for setting me free from the pattern of the world and the patterns of my life and for shifting me into Your paradigm of living free!

Self-reconciliation:

[Say your name], you are free...abundantly free. You are filled with the Holy Spirit who causes you to walk in freedom. Every chain that hinders you is broken in Jesus' name, and there is no thought or emotion that ties you down or impedes you. Skip, jump, and shout...for you are free!

Passage:

"And the Lord will make you the head and not the tail; you shall be above only, and not be beneath, If you heed the commandments of the Lord your God, which I command you today, and are careful to observe them." (Deut. 28:13 NKJV)

Declaration:

Oh, what a blessing to know that I am the head and not the tail. I declare that I am not wagged by the world, but that I have authority. I am not a victim of all that is around me. I am only subject to the Holy Spirit within me. I rejoice in the partnership that You have given me... to walk in victory and have dominion. things of this world have no control over me, my thoughts have no control over me, and my emotions have no control over me. I declare obedience in my life, and I surrender my all to Your all, therefore, I am not driven by life, but rather I navigate life by the Holy Spirit and design the life You have blessed me to live!

Self-reconciliation:

[Say your name], you are the head and not the tail and nothing rattles you. In all things, in all thoughts, in all emotions, you stand firmly and are only guided by the Holy Spirit. You are not driven by the winds and the waves of the world. You flow according to the movement of the kingdom. Today, you will design the life you want to live as you surrender to the voice of the Holy Spirit and obey His direction. You will end the day confident in your authority in Christ!

Chapter Five
Renewing Your Mind

What does it look like to renew the mind? I think we recognize the fact that we need to have our minds renewed (Romans 12:2) and we acknowledge there are great effects that come from the process, but what does that mean for us on a daily basis? Remember, this book is to do more than just give you information or tell you how to do something. In these next chapters, I hope to walk you through some very practical exercises that will equip you to renew your mind and enforce your God-design. You might want to grab a notebook and take time to stop and walk yourself through some of them!

WHAT IF YOU'RE LIVING A LIE?

I believe that one of the biggest things that keeps people from thinking like God and embracing His truth is that fact that we think we already know it. Moreover, we also think we are living how He wants us to live. I recently preached in a local church and title of the message was "If you were living a lie, would you want to know?" We simply don't know what we don't know. Think for a moment: Would you want to know what you might not know? This would require admitting that you could be wrong, or that your understanding might be incomplete; that there could be something different or something more. I firmly believe that our existing knowledge is our greatest obstacle to learning. Likewise, our existing beliefs often are the biggest lies that keep us from truth. We are so convinced that we already know truth, that sometimes we miss truth.

Think about Pontius Pilate in John 18:38. He looked at Jesus and said, "What is truth?" He was staring into the face of truth, yet he didn't see it. Crazy! Even more, he asked the question and then turned and walked out, without even waiting for an answer. We can only assume it is because he thought he already knew the answer, and it was the answer that he adopted from his system around him. His current knowledge of what he believed kept him from learning THE Answer. There was something he didn't know that he didn't know.

The Jews also missed an opportunity to hear and know truth in John 8:32&33:

> *"And you shall know the truth, and the truth shall make you free." They answered Him, "We are Abraham's descendants, and have never been in bondage to anyone. How can You say, 'You will be made free'?"*

Jesus presented the Jews with an opportunity to walk in the freedom of truth...His truth. Just like He presented truth to the woman at the well. But instead of considering that He was offering them a paradigm shift, they allowed the paradigm of their system and experience to blind them from what they didn't know. And they responded incredulously by saying, "When have we ever been in captivity?" They allowed their current knowledge to keep them from considering that there could be something more to know.

From my perspective, this response seems ludicrous. We can read the entire history of the Jews in the Old Testament and learn that it was all about bondage and captivity. From the Egyptians, to the Assyrians, to the Babylonians, to the Romans (of whom they were presently in captivity)... all they knew was captivity! This was their story (the sum total of their system and their experience); it was their reality and they equated their reality with truth... even though it was a lie.

This is too often the case with us. We make our reality our truth, but that doesn't mean that it IS true, it just means that it is your reality! I cannot say this enough because I really want you to get it!

I deal with this every day when people come into our program or in for counseling. So many define their very existence according to the realities they have lived. When I say, "Tell me a bit about you," they spend the next hour telling me all about their story. Now, your story can explain a lot of why you are the way you are, the problem is, too often, we allow it to write who we are becoming. Too many people have already predetermined their tomorrow based on their past. More specifically, they predetermine their tomorrow on what they have determined their past says about them. In other words, they allow the definitions of their past to define their future. If the past says, "You are rejected," then they too often assume the future says, "You will be rejected." If the past says, "You are poor," then we assume that prosperity must not be in the cards. Therefore, we settle for survival decisions that keep us stuck in poverty instead of considering that poverty, albeit your reality, does not equal your truth.

DO YOU WANT TO KNOW
WHAT YOU DON'T KNOW?

So, here's the real question:

If you were living a lie, would you want to know?

Answering this question is the very first step to opening your eyes to see what you have been blind to and consider that maybe there is something you don't know.

After healing a blind man in John 9:41, Jesus addresses the Pharisees by saying,

> *"Jesus said to them, 'If you were blind, you would have no sin; but now you say, 'We see.' Therefore your sin remains.'"*

The Pharisees were the leaders in the synagogues and were educated in the laws of Judaism. Unfortunately, their knowledge of religion kept them from learning and receiving something that was outside of their understanding. I would like to propose that too often, worldly wisdom misses out on spiritual revelation; it clouds the mind's spiritual eye.

The word *blind* in verse 41 in Greek includes the idea of being mentally blind, being unable to see in the mind, or a lack of understanding. It also denotes the idea of a fog. Interesting that this is what Jesus is referring to when he addressed the Pharisees. He was saying that because they tried to comprehend everything through the mind, they would never see the supernatural work of God. If they would "blind" their minds, they would finally see in the spirit and recognize that the blind man was healed only by the hand of God. In their search for intellectual understanding (along with their disdain of the Sabbath being broken), they missed out on the miracle. Their existing knowledge of God actually kept them from seeing God!

I am reminded of Simeon in Luke 2. The Bible says he was "just and devout" and the Holy Spirit was upon him. It had been revealed to Simeon by the Holy Spirit that "he would not see death before he had seen the Lord's Christ" (Luke 2:26). This is the core belief that predetermined his encounter with Jesus.

> *"And when the parents brought in the Child Jesus, to do for Him according to the custom of the law, he (Simeon) took Him up in his arms and blessed God and said: 'Lord, now You are letting Your servant depart in peace, According to Your word; for my eyes have seen Your salvation." (Luke 2:27-30 NKJV)*

Scripture doesn't reveal this part, but I can imagine that there were likely many people in the temple that day, yet only one recognized the work of God, while it was still in infancy. Many of us miss miracles and works of God when they are full blown in our face! How wonderful that he saw it in an infantile state. This is too often because we are watching with our mind instead of by the Holy Spirit. Simply said, your intellect and preconceived ideas will often cloud your spiritual vision and will cause you to miss miracles, moreover, you will miss prophetic fulfillments and promises!

So again I ask, "You don't know what you don't know, but do you want to know what you might not know?"

CORE LIES

> *"He feeds on ashes; a deceived heart hath turned him aside, that he cannot deliver his soul, nor say, is there not a lie in my right hand?" (Isaiah 44:20 NKJV)*

This verse is a reminder that we all struggle with core lies that feed into who we become. And, even though it may feel as though those lies have a hold on our hearts and minds, it is important to note that this verse states that we are actually holding onto them! A core lie feels so captivating because our flesh or our personality often get molded around that lie, and it becomes "a part of us." This is why we often don't recognize the lie, even though we are gripping it so tightly with our hands! Furthermore, to think about letting go of that lie can feel frightening because it means we "lose" a part of who we are and the comfort of the familiarity of the lie. We know what to expect and we know how to respond; it is our norm, albeit often a miserable norm.

Many of you might be reading this right now and thinking, "I don't have any lies. I have been set free from them all." Well, remember, you don't know what you don't know, and if you think you don't have any core lies, you could be deceived. Be willing to recognize that many negative emotions, thoughts, or behaviors are typically tied to a core lie.

IDENTIFYING CORE LIES

One of the first steps to embracing truth is to identify any core lies present in your system. Core lies can also be limiting beliefs. These can be ideas or concepts, information or knowledge that keeps you from receiving and moving into truth. When trying to identify core lies with my clients, I might ask these questions:

- How would you describe yourself?
- How would others describe you?
- If God walked in the room, how would He describe you?

This is to expose the many different opinions of how they would be described or defined. Then I will ask these questions:

- Which description do you agree with the most?
- Which one are you most influenced by?

This is to expose where they are unreconciled with their God-design. In other words, when we agree with or are influenced by any definition of who we are more than God's definition, we are not reconciled with who we are in Christ. This is a good way to add God to the equation.

Remember, our core beliefs have become the sum of life's "inputs." We learned earlier that your system + your experience = your belief, which ultimately becomes your paradigm. But what happens when I add an addend to an addition equation? It changes the answer, or the outcome. Likewise, when I add something or in this case someone, to this equation, the answer and outcome is altered... shifted... transformed... renewed!

This is what I am doing when I am asking the questions above; I am inserting Jesus and His opinion about you into the equation.

MY SYSTEM + MY EXPERIENCE
+ JESUS = A PARADIGM SHIFT

By adding Jesus into any circumstance, we expose where our beliefs are not in line with truth. In order to align ourselves, we must shift our mind into agreement with His. This will often cause a crisis of belief, where we have to decide in a moment, "What will I choose to believe?" Or more practically, "What will I choose to do?" There will be more on this in the next chapter, but let's talk about emotions for a moment.

EMOTIONS ARE ROAD SIGNS

Although identifying your core lies goes deeper than dealing with your emotions, it is important to know that your emotions play a big part in the process. Behind every emotion, there is a belief. We could say that the belief is the "why" of the emotion. I often ask my clients why they think they feel a particular way or what thought is connected to an emotion they express. This will often help identify the belief that is behind the emotion.

Consider that emotions are like road signs that can navigate you to a final destination. Road signs are not the final destination, they are not the stopping point. Rather, they simply give information that is pertinent to where you want to be. Likewise, emotions can be viewed as data that points you to a core belief. In this manner, emotions can be helpful. Like road signs, they are an important part of the journey and help navigate you to understand your values and core beliefs. They also reveal this same thing in others. However, too often we allow emotions to drive us instead of using them to inform us and help us "self-discover" what is within us.

So there is a balance here that needs to be learned. Too often we are taught to control our emotions, which we take to mean, "squelch them, ignore them, stuff them, or pretend they don't exist." But we would not do that with road signs that are intentionally placed so we don't get lost in our journey. We don't ignore signs. We shouldn't ignore emotions.

However, we also would not park in front of a road sign and stay there. If you don't move past a road sign, you never get to the destination. Likewise, some never move beyond an emotion. On this end of the spectrum are people who never moved past their emotions but consider them a part of who they are. They can't seem to separate the feeling from the feeler and don't recognize that we are not our emotions, we simply have emotions.

I think it is important to note that there is no such thing as a negative emotion; after all, emotions are a part of our God-design. Where the emotion is rooted and what you do with the emotion is where we often go wrong. When we allow the emotion itself to control us, that can be negative. However, if an emotion is rooted on a belief that is truth, it can often be the fire or passion behind why we do what we do. I say this because I am a very passionate person and very emotionally driven...which is what gives me fire for what I do. I strive to harness my emotions instead of being harnessed by my emotions. I can very easily be derailed if I am not intentional to keep my emotions rooted in Christ. Otherwise, the emotion can become like a wild bull, and I end up feeling unstable, insecure, and out of control.

This is why it is important to be emotionally

aware. Emotions can be a great strength or a great weakness. It is not about trying to squelch emotions. It is about learning how to recognize them and navigate through them.

The Bible tells us that a sign of a believer is that we "take up serpents" (Mark 16:18). I believe this is referring to the power that we must grab a hold of—emotions that could poison us—and handle them with authority. It's like pulling anger out of your heart and saying, "Anger, you will no longer handle me, but I will handle you!" Psychologists might call this emotional agility, educators might refer to this as emotional intelligence, but I like to refer to it as emotional authority. Call it what you want, renewing the mind starts by being emotionally aware, understanding the thoughts (beliefs) behind emotions, and then recognizing the pattern we have established because of them.

Keep reading. The next chapter is going to peel back a layer and walk you through this process more intentionally. I want you to be equipped to walk in your empowerment and understand what it looks like to start enforcing YOU!

Prayer Practice:
Father, I thank You for revealing the places in my life where I have been bound and blinded by lies. I seek You, God, and Your light, and I ask You to continue to illuminate places in my life where I am living in lies. I want to know You, and I ask You to open my eyes to see the way You see. Help me to recognize the emotions

and thoughts in my life that are leading me to a deeper understanding of who I am and what I am founded upon. I am not afraid to seek out my emotions and discover what they are rooted in. I desire to be founded only upon Your truth. I am expecting that as I allow You to search my heart and mind, that by Your Holy Spirit and Your navigation, I will be freed from lies and brought into Your truth. I declare that every lie is being exposed and that day by day, I am coming more and more into Your truth. In Jesus' name I pray, amen.

Enforcing You

Passage:

"For the word of God is living and powerful, and sharper than any two-edged sword, piercing even to the division of soul and spirit, and of joints and marrow, and is a discerner of the thoughts and intents of the heart. And there is no creature hidden from His sight, but all things are naked and open to the eyes of Him to whom we must give account."
(Hebrews 4:12-13 NKJV)

Declaration:

God, thank You that Your Word separates the things that are of the soul from the things that are of the Spirit. I declare that as I read Your Word, I can clearly discern my own thoughts and intents that are of my flesh versus those of Your Spirit. Thank You that I am seen by You and that Your eyes see my inmost being. That I am open to Your eyes and I recognize that to You and You alone I give account. I declare that Your Word is revealing things in my life that are not in the fullness of Your truth and that by Your truth I am being set free from all deception.

Self-reconciliation:

[Say your name], You are growing in the discernment of your own soul as you saturate yourself in the Word. Because of His Word, you are able to separate what is of your soul and what is of the Spirit. You are not confused but rather His Word lights up your inside and you see it the way God sees it. There is no covering, there is no mask. You are laid bare, and you are free in your nakedness. You feel no account to the world or to man; your only concern is with the Lord and His Truth for your life. You are free from internal tension, for His Word is written in your heart and you are confident in His discernment of every thought and intent you have.

Passage:

"But as it is written:
'Eye has not seen, nor ear heard,
Nor have entered into the heart of man
The things which God has prepared for those who love Him.'
But God has revealed them to us through His Spirit. For the Spirit searches all things, yes, the deep things of God." (1Cor 2:9-10 NKJV)

Declaration:

I once was blind, I once was deaf, I once was lost, but I declare that by Your Spirit, my eye now sees, my ear now hears, and my purpose is made clear. My heart is in line with Yours and I am understanding the lies that hold me from Your fullness. You have revealed truth to me, and I declare that what I once did not know, I now know. Your truth has indeed set me free!

Self-reconciliation:

[Say your name], you have the Spirit of God in you that gives you Spiritual sight and hearing. You do see, and you do hear! There is a kingdom fire that burns in your heart and you have a deep "knowing in your knower." For the things which God has prepared for you have entered into your heart and the deep things of God are within you.

Passage:

"Search me, O God, and know my heart; Try me, and know my anxieties; And see if there is any wicked way in me, And lead me in the way everlasting." (Psalm 139:23-24 NKJV)

Declaration:

I open my heart and mind to You, God, for You to examine and search. Reveal any fears, worries, or emotions that would lead me down a path that is less than your blessed path. Help me to recognize emotions that are connected to core lies and show me where my values and beliefs do not line up with Yours. I rejoice in the cleansing power of Your Holy Spirit that frees me from all manners of wickedness.

Self-reconciliation:

[Say your name], you are led in the way of everlasting as you allow the Holy Spirit to search all that is within you. All manners of wickedness and all anxieties, worries, and fears are being revealed to you and His truth is cleansing you as you receive it.

Passage:

"Watch and pray, lest you enter into temptation. The spirit indeed is willing, but the flesh is weak." (Matthew 26:41 NKJV)

Declaration:

God, You are all too familiar with the weaknesses of my flesh. My emotions will cause me to stumble if I am not intentional to watch over them and pray into them. Thank You that by Your spirit, I am strong, and You know that in my heart, I desire to stay out of my flesh and walk in Your truth. I agree with You and declare that my spirit is indeed willing, and I am standing guard, watching and praying over my flesh. I will not give in to temptation but will stand strong in my spirit.

Self-reconciliation

[Say your name], your spirit is never unwilling. You are always ready and wanting to walk in righteousness. You are aware of your flesh and girded up in prayer and you will not enter into temptation. You stand strong and overcome the weakness of your flesh!

Passage:

"Blessed is the man
who walks not in the counsel of the wicked,
nor stands in the way of sinners,
nor sits in the seat of scoffers;
but his delight is in the law of the Lord,
and on his law he meditates day and night."
(Psalm 1:1-2 NKJV)

Declaration:

Thank You, Lord, for instructing me by Your Law and putting in me a desire to meditate on it day and night. I declare that by Your Word, I am filled with delight and I walk in Your blessings. I declare and decree that I do not entertain the ways of the world, I am entertained by Your Presence through Your Word. I receive the blessing in Jesus' name!

Self-reconciliation:

[Say your name], you are a blessed woman because you delight in the law of God. Your heart is set upon His ways and you are focused on His heart. I speak the meditations of the Spirit over you... that even while you sleep, you are pondering His love. You have no interest in the ways of the world, and you are content with His truths. You have great confidence in His love.

Chapter Six
Intentional Processing

Let's go back for a minute to examining habits. With every stimulus, there is a response. Likewise, for every emotion or thought, there is a response. Unfortunately, over time, often the emotion or thought become synonymous with the response, meaning, there is no "space" or "gap" between the two. We could say it becomes more like a trigger and a reaction, or a "triggered reaction." In other words, how you react becomes habitual because of the neural pathway that has been developed. And remember, a habit requires very little effort or thinking; there is no need to process through it.

An example is when I feel anger and without thinking I punch something or someone. Without thinking, the action comes almost as if it is attached to the emotion itself. Interesting to note that often we might use the verbiage, "That made me mad," or "She made me mad," thus giving our authority over our emotions over to another person or circumstance. Nonetheless, it is fair to say that often we become enslaved or victimized by our own habits because we feel stuck in the rut of that behavior or kneejerk reaction. But is that true? Absolutely not! It just means that we have identified an area where we must be intentional to renew the mind and practice new behaviors.

It is important to note that "triggered reactions" are conditioned behaviors. We have conditioned ourselves (or have been conditioned) that a particular stimulus requires a particular response (like Pavlov's dog). This is good news because with a little "reconditioning," we can change our toxic behaviors. This is what it means to renew the mind... to recondition the way we think and intentionally process something, thus causing a change in our responses.

WIDENING THE GAP

Let's talk about how to be intentional, to widen that gap and put space between the stimulus and the response. This requires recognizing the emotion or thought at the onset, but then taking a moment to look beyond the emotion into the *why* behind it. This is where we start to identify core beliefs, more importantly, beliefs (core lies) that are not in alignment with the truth of what God says. In short, learning to widen the gap brings awareness to core lies and empowers you to attack and rewrite them!

JESUS WIDENS THE GAP

I love the story in John chapter 8 when we learn of a woman caught in the act of adultery. She is brought to Jesus for "judgment." Now, I can only imagine the hype of this scene as she is dragged through the streets while people yelled, criticized, and condemned her for her actions. Not only was adultery considered immoral, but it was against the law, and such a crime was deserving of stoning. This value system caused such emotions of rage and hatred! No doubt there was intensity in the crowd as they expected justice to be paid. But watch how Jesus captures this moment and widens the gap between the stimulus (the woman's behavior) and the response (how He would answer their question).

> *"They said to Him, 'Teacher, this woman was caught in adultery, in the very act. Now Moses, in the law, commanded us that such should be stoned, But what do You say?'* **...But Jesus stooped down and wrote on the ground with His finger, as though He did not hear."** *(John 8:4-6 NKJV, emphasis mine)*

O man, o man! I can only imagine how that irritated the scribes and Pharisees. No doubt they were relying on the emotion of the people and the urgency of the situation to stir up a reaction out of Jesus. But the Bible tells us that Jesus nonchalantly stooped down and began to doodle in the dirt on the ground as if He didn't hear a word. Talk about feeling ignored, dismissed, and invisible! Jesus caused a hush to come over the hype; His actions pushed the pause button on the scene and brought it to complete halt. Talk about taking authority! He literally shifted the entire scene by putting space between the question and the answer!

This is how we create space between the stimulus and the response. Some of us would do well to learn how to stop and doodle for a moment and "tune out" the voice of the circumstance and the emotions of the people involved. We need to learn to push the pause button on our emotions, our thoughts, the opinions, and voices of those around us. Take a breath and breathe! Get a pencil out and doodle for a bit and step into the authority you have in Christ to shift the scenes of your life!

Let me break it down even more for you. When I am dealing with clients, I typically teach them these steps to walk them through how to widen the gap between your emotions and your actions.

Remember these five words: Define, Identify, Decide, Declare, and Do! Learning to intentionally process these steps is hugely empowering and will make you more aware of why you do what you do, why you feel what you feel, but more importantly, how to change what you do and how you feel. This is the authority that God has given to you to walk in victory and not become victimized by your thoughts and emotions. By learning and doing these steps, you will cause the gap between your triggers and reactions to widen and you will begin to recognize stimuli and choose better responses.

DEFINE

The first step is to define, "What am I feeling?" This seems easy, but if you have ever been in a storm of emotions, you know that isn't always the case. I often will ask my clients who are in a moment of surging emotions, "If you were going to text me an emoji, which one would you pick?" With kiddos, I have a chart of faces that I let them look at to help them really narrow their emotions and define what they are feeling. (The chart works well with men, too!) It is important to note every feeling you might be experiencing, then try to narrow it down as much as possible to one or two. This is where a counselor (or friend) might ask really good questions to help you discover what your foundational emotion is. This is usually what somebody is doing when they are verbally processing their emotions; they are looking for the source. Typically, all of our feelings are rooted in one foundational emotion, and that is what we are looking for. This is where we begin to recognize core lies because you will see the pattern of all your "junk" coming back to the same emotion.

> *"The lamp of the Eternal illuminates the human spirit, searching our most intimate thoughts."*
> *(Proverbs 20:27 The Voice Translation)*

> *"Explore me, O God, and know the real me. Dig deeply and discover who I am. Put me to the test and watch how I handle the strain."*
> *(Psalm 139:23 The Voice Translation)*

It is important to invite the Holy Spirit into this process and allow Him to search your soul. No one knows the heart better than God and He has a way of highlighting what we might otherwise miss or dismiss. Things that are the norm for us can actually be toxic feelings or thoughts and we could actually be living a lie. Remember, we don't know what we don't know. So while I mentioned that a counselor could help in that discovery process, there is no counselor like The Wonderful Counselor! (Isaiah 9:6) This is the value in pursuing intimacy with God when we are working through emotions and thoughts. He indeed digs deeper than we, or any counselor, would dig without His guidance. But most importantly, He is loving and gentle in all His ways. Even in correction, there is love!

IDENTIFY

Every emotion is rooted in a thought. That was why the section about road signs was so important. Remember, my emotion is going to reveal a core belief. So once we have defined the emotion I am feeling in a moment, I want to identify the "why" behind it. Questions like: "What was happening when you first noticed this emotion start to 'pop up'?" or "What triggered this emotion?" or "Why do you think you feel this way?" or "What message are you hearing that has triggered this emotion?" or "What message did you hear in that experience?"

These questions will help peel back the emotion and look deeper into your mind and your core beliefs. They not only help reveal the trigger, but also why it is a trigger. This is where we see how intertwined the mind and the emotions really are. Some people can more easily identify the why before they define the emotion. "Thinkers" can usually define what they are thinking, while "feelers" define what they are feeling. For this purpose, you may have to bop back and forth until you go as deep into the root as possible. That's OK! Either way we end up at the same place: Understanding what am I feeling and why.

So this process looks so far like:

"I don't want to be around my mom!"
"What do you think is the reason for that...?"
"I don't know..."
"What do you think is your strongest emotion when you think about your mom?"
"...maybe anger...?"
"When do you think this anger started...?"
"After my party..."
"So, how is your party connected to your anger?"

"My mom didn't show up to my party."
"Is it fair to say that you are angry because your mom didn't show up to your party?"
"Yes..."
"Why do you think your mom's absence triggered anger?"
"Because it was my birthday and my mom should be there!"
"So what message are you hearing from your

mom by her not showing up?"

"...that I am not worth her time, that I am not important..."

"So you feel angry because you don't feel worthy or important?"

"Yes!"

This person likely feels unworthy and unimportant in many aspects of her life. Furthermore, she likely has become one with her emotions; the feeler has actually "become" the feeling. This means the feeling defines her. Statements like, "I am unworthy" and "I am unimportant" reveal that the feeler has actually taken on the feeling as a part of her identity.

A better statement is, "I am struggling with the feeling of unworthiness." Or "I feel unimportant." This identifies the emotion and the reality of it but doesn't allow the emotion to identify you. That said, let's go back to the dialogue above. The original issue was a desire to disconnect from her mom. We were able to define the emotion tied to that choice—anger. However, anger is not really the issue (and frankly neither is her mom). Anger is the symptom or the result, and her mom is the trigger! The anger is the pattern of behavior or the paradigm this person lives in, and her mom is likely a nerve around this issue (or perhaps a part of the system that established the paradigm), but neither of them are the root of the issue. The issue here is a core lie, which in this case is likely "I am unworthy" or "I am unimportant."

Now, this is where we begin to see the empowerment we can walk in when we choose not to allow others to be the cause of our emotions. To say, "Mom made me mad," is to say, "Mom has emotional power over me." Is that Mom's fault? Or yours? Hear me when I say that our past and the people in it (our system and our experiences) can explain some of the brokenness in our paradigm, but when we allow them to become our excuse, we forfeit our God-given authority.

> "Now let Us conceive a new creation—humanity—made in Our image, fashioned according to Our likeness. And let Us grant them authority over all the earth..."
> (Genesis 1:26 The Voice Translation)

> "Now you understand that I have imparted to you all my authority to trample over his kingdom. You will trample upon every demon before you and overcome every power Satan possesses. Absolutely nothing will be able to harm you as you walk in this authority."
> (Luke 10:19 The Passion Translation)

In Christ, we have been given the authority to practice His power over any stronghold. This includes the strongholds of our core beliefs. A stronghold can be a place where we settle and find respite, or it can be a place that holds us captive. When our system and experience build in us core beliefs that are contrary to the freedom and authority of Jesus, it is a lie... period! Don't hand over your authority, take ownership and be delivered. This is where the next step comes in... decide.

DECIDE

Now we have defined and identified what we are feeling and why. We have found the root, which remember typically reveals our core lie! Now, we have to decide what we want to do with that core lie. At this point you get to step into the authority of Jesus and navigate how you will respond and create space between the stimulus and the reaction. It is so empowering when you learn to capture thoughts and emotions in a moment and realize that you don't have to respond the way you always have—you have options! The enemy always wants you to feel victimized or "stuck." He wants you to feel as if "you have no choice." How many times I hear someone say, "Well, I *have* to..." or "I don't really have a choice..." or we give credit to others for the choices we make saying, "She made me mad" or "He made me angry." We have completely stepped out of the freedom of the Spirit and made ourselves captive to a lie. As I mentioned before, blaming others will never set you free. Instead, you must decide you are going to take ownership of how you choose to think or feel in a moment and how you are going to deal with what you think or feel. I say that because sometimes, our feelings or thoughts are so real, we can't stop feeling or thinking... but we can decide how we are going to deal with them.

I tell my clients that feelings in and of themselves are not wrong, it is what triggers them and what we do with them that typically causes us to stumble. We have talked about discovering the trigger, now we have to decide what we want to do.

Let's revisit the statement I made earlier...

MY SYSTEM + MY EXPERIENCE + JESUS =
A PARADIGM SHIFT

By adding Jesus into any circumstance, we expose where our beliefs are not in line with truth. In order to align ourselves, we must shift our mind into agreement with His. This will often cause a crisis of belief, where we have to decide in a moment, "What will I choose to believe?" Or more practically, "What will I choose to do?"

Once you have defined what you are feeling and have identified why you are feeling it, it is time to compare your existing paradigm to God's paradigm. There is no standard like the standard of the Lord...He is the Plumb Line (Amos 7) by which we measure what is true and not true and upon which we build a life that is able to stand amid stormy trials. Isaiah said that when the enemy comes in like a flood, "the Spirit of the Lord will lift up a standard against him" (Is. 59:19). We cannot fight with our own opinions or persuasions. Nor can the opinions of others completely set us free from the lies that hold us captive. While we might be able to experience temporary relief, it is only by the Spirit of the Lord that our minds can be completely transformed. I am not interested in teaching you how to be relieved of your emotions and thoughts, or even how to manage them, I am interested in total deliverance from everything that holds you captive to anything less than His confidence and freedom.

So what does this process look like? Once you have defined what you are feeling or thinking, and you have identified what triggered it, allow God to enter into your thought process and ask Him what *He* thinks or feels about the message you believe or emotion you are feeling. Chances are, what He will say in the moment is different than what you are hearing, believing, or saying to yourself. Then ask yourself, "What do I choose to believe?" or "Who do I choose to believe?" This is where you must decide if you will believe what your feelings are telling you. Will you believe what reality is speaking? Will you believe what that person just said? Will you believe your own opinion of the circumstance? Or, will you believe God? Here's the deal, there is no in-between, you either believe Him or you don't!

> *"Adulterers and adulteresses! Do you not know that friendship with the world is enmity with God? Whoever therefore wants to be a friend of the world makes himself an enemy of God."*
> *(James 4:4 NKJV)*

This is why the prophet Elijah said to the prophets of Baal, "How long will you falter between two opinions? If the Lord *is* God, follow Him; but if Baal, follow him" (1Kings 18:21). They were held to the opinion of the world that kept them bowing to a false god. We may not realize it, but too often we serve everything but the one true God. To believe another word is to become controlled and captivated by that word.

It is very important to note that at this point, you are either in agreement with God or you are not. Choosing to agree with your own conclusion, the conclusion of others, or the conclusion of your circumstance is in disagreement with God, and this is YOUR sin. This is the point where repentance is imperative in breaking off the lie that you have been stuck in. You cannot miss this step because repentance is the key to deliverance of any particular stronghold. It is the power that you hold to set yourself free. Where you first received your lie may not be your doing but holding on to it is!

> *"If we confess our sins, He is faithful and just to forgive us our sins and to cleanse us from all unrighteousness." (1 John 1:9 NKJV)*

Through this process, we are able to shed light where our soul is not reconciled with truth. The areas where we hold on to thoughts, beliefs, and emotions that are not in line with God must be acknowledged and confessed as sin.

Let's continue with our example from above:

"You feel that you are unimportant and lack value?"

"Yes."

"Is that true?"

"Well, it must be true, or my mom would have come to my party."

"What would God say?"

"What do you mean?"

"Would He say you are unimportant? Would He agree that you have no value?"

"Probably not."

"Do you believe that God sees you as valuable?"

"Yes, but I don't feel valuable."

"I understand, but I am not asking you what you feel...I am asking you what you choose to believe. Do you believe the message of your mom and your mind, or do you believe God?"

I have handed all authority over to this person. This is no longer about her mom, her anger, or her rejection; this is now about what she chooses to believe. Will she say that the judgment of man is greater than the judgment of God? God has made His judgment on the cross and it is always rooted in love. That is never in question. The only question is what will you choose to believe?

Now, I would likely attack this core lie a step further to address the need this person has for the approval and love from man (in this case, Mom).

"The Bible says He will never leave you...
what do you think that means?"
"I don't really know?"
"Do you think He was there with you at your
party?"
"Well, I guess He was."
"How can knowing that God is always with
you change the impact rejection has on you in
a moment? Is His presence and love enough
for you? Do you want it to be your only source
and be rid of the feeling of rejection and
anger?"

I am just showing you how I might go deeper
to really address some core lies within the heart of
this individual. This exposes why it is so important to
practice God's truth and reconcile His Word with the
words in your head.

By choosing to believe God, you make the
decision to surrender your thoughts and beliefs to
Him. This is when it gets so empowering. I get to say
to myself, "What do I decide to do with this rejection?
This anger? This belief that I am unimportant?"

I would also likely guide this person to
confess where she has put the need for her mother's
acceptance above the acceptance of God. In other
words, her mother has the throne in her heart in that
she controls her daughter's emotions and beliefs.
This might look like this...

"I confess that the love and acceptance of my

mom has controlled how I feel and I have allowed anger to settle in my heart because of rejection. I recognize that I am not rejected, and I agree with Your love and acceptance. I confess that I have allowed my mom's love to mean more to me than Your love, and I break that lie right now in the name of Jesus."

You might be thinking, geez, this seems a little extreme, but justifying your negative emotions is choosing to live a lie. I ask you, if you were living a lie, would you want to know? More importantly, would you be willing to take ownership in order to be set free? Ignorance may be bliss, but it isn't freedom. It is possible that by not dealing with your emotions, or by simply justifying or managing them, you have missed out on being set free from a core lie that has long held you captive. Well, it is time to take that which has held you captive and drag it into submission to the truth.

"For though we walk in the flesh, we do not war according to the flesh. For the weapons of our warfare are not carnal but mighty in God for pulling down strongholds, casting down arguments and every high thing that exalts itself against the knowledge of God, bringing every thought into captivity to the obedience of Christ" (2 Cor. 10:5 NKJV)

Those thoughts that are trying to trump (exalt

themselves over) the truth of Christ must be cast down and brought into the obedience of Jesus. Once we recognize them, we must choose to submit those thoughts to God and then declare the Word over them. That is our weapon of warfare.

DECLARE

My favorite part is declaring truth because it is so incredibly empowering. By declaring truth, we shift emotions, thoughts, opinions, circumstances, relationships, etc. into the status of being completely irrelevant. At this point, all that matters is what truth says! There is refreshment and quiet that takes place when we are told where to "land the plane." In other words, settling your emotions, thoughts, and opinions on a given truth. No more considering, no more wondering, no more internal tension, no more thinking, no more reasoning, no more conflict... just simply declaring what is true despite it all!

My job primarily consists of making decisions, working through conflicts, finding solutions, and putting out fires. The mental and emotional energy of thinking through every situation can be exhausting. Especially when you are not sure of where you choose to land the plane. For this purpose, when Brad and I go on vacations, I make it clear that I don't want to make decisions. He knows what I like, and he knows what I don't like. I am sure that he is going to put together a schedule of events that is satisfying and pleasing to me. Not having to think or make decisions is very refreshing and freeing... it is often the much-needed break that I need.

This is what I am talking about regarding the freedom that comes with declaring truth. It is like the much-needed break that we need from our own emotions and thoughts!

Now the concept of declaring truth has already been sprinkled throughout this whole process of widening the gap, but it is necessary to make a point of talking about it. Up until now, we have primarily talked about defining, identifying, and deciding, and all of those things are necessary, but it is only the implantation of Word of God that actually sanctifies your soul (James 1:21). This is the step that takes you beyond training or re-training the mind and into the supernatural power having your mind transformed.

> *"And do not be conformed to this world, but be transformed by the renewing of your mind, that you may prove what is that good and acceptable and perfect will of God."*
> *(Romans 12:2 NKJV)*

This verse tells us that transformation comes by *renewing* the mind. The word renewing used in this verse is a derivative of the word *renovate*. When we renovate something, we are giving it a completely new look; out with the old, and in with the new! We live in a world filled with stimuli—things that threaten to trigger us. We cannot change that, but we can change the way we respond by changing the way we think. Remember...

> "Your core beliefs predetermine how you perceive, what your perspective is, and ultimately what your paradigm (your reality) will become."

This is why declaring the Word is so important. It is how you cleanse your mind of lies and convince yourself of truth. Call it a form of brainwashing if you want. My brain needs a regular washing, and so does my heart, for that matter! I have to stay saturated in truth by girding up with His armor or I will waver in times of emotional and mental battles.

This is what it means to put on the armor of God before you go into battle:

> *"Therefore take up the whole armor of God, that you may be able to withstand in the evil day, and having done all, to stand."*
> *(Ephesians 6:13 NKJV)*

No one waits to throw their armor on until they are in the midst of battle. The armor is what *prepares* them for battle. You and I are in a battle against the wiles of the devil and how he has deceived our minds. But praise God that there is victory in Jesus. We have been given the mind of Christ (1 Cor. 2:16), but we must be intentional to "put it on!" This is what you do when you declare

117

Scriptures in your life. You are literally rewriting your thoughts and beliefs by adorning yourself with new truths. Just like changing your clothes, you are taking off an old outfit and replacing it with a new one. This is why the "Enforcing YOU" sections at the end of each chapter are such a crucial part of this book! It is walking you through how to declare and access the mind of Christ. I pray that you have not skipped or even skimmed them. If you have, you are missing out on how much God wants to do to revolutionize your life!

David was excellent at declaring truth into his life. I would highly recommend reading Psalm 42 through the lens of this entire chapter, but for the sake of bringing home the example of declaring truth, take a look at verse 5:

"Why are you cast down, O my soul?
And why are you disquieted within me?
Hope in God, for I shall yet praise Him
For the help of His countenance."

In this single phrase, David defines what he is feeling (downcast and disquieted), identifies why (he has lost hope), and then we hear him declaring a decision into his own soul. "I will hope, I will praise, I will place my hope in Your countenance!" Not once, but twice he declares this, once in verse 5 and then again in verse 11. Why? Because he is battling in his soul... his thinking is unstable and his emotions are sinking. David knew it was imperative to stand on what is true. He knew that only God's truth could overcome the weaknesses of his flesh.

> *"Deep calls unto deep at the noise of Your waterfalls;*
> *All Your waves and billows have gone over me." (verse 7)*

David counted on God's voice to speak louder than the rumble of his own voice in his head. This was his hope when his emotions wanted to lead him to core lies of hopelessness!

Throughout this entire psalm, David flies the plane of his emotions all over the place. He is honest with himself and faces what he is feeling and why, but in the end, he chose to land the plane on truth and spoke it boldly with a robust declaration in verse 8.

> *"The Lord will command His loving kindness in the daytime,*
> *And in the night His song shall be with me—*
> *A prayer to the God of my life." (verse 8)*

How is it that David was so sure? How is it that he was so confident in God? Regardless of what he felt, he chose to be sure and he chose to believe! His declaration of truth emboldened him to make that choice... you might say he "brainwashed" himself.

DO

The last step is "Do." This is an action word

calling you to do something that supports what you have decided and declared. Without action, words are just words. You start with words, but end with action. The Bible is filled with exhortations to add actions to words. It tells us continually that without action, there is no stability. Our words are solidified by actions.

> *"Therefore whoever hears these sayings of Mine, and does them, I will liken him to a wise man who built his house on the rock: and the rain descended, the floods came, and the winds blew and beat on that house; and it did not fall, for it was founded on the rock.*
>
> *"But everyone who hears these sayings of Mine, and does not do them, will be like a foolish man who built his house on the sand: and the rain descended, the floods came, and the winds blew and beat on that house; and it fell. And great was its fall."*
> *(Matthew 7:24-27 NKJV)*

The key phrase in this verse is: *"and does them."* The Greek phraseology used means to execute, carry out, to keep, or to perform. It also denotes the idea of making, producing, or authoring a thing. I believe this is what it means to "faith it until you become it." Even in what might be absent in your reality, if we act as though it exists, then it does exist... the truth will become your reality! Think about it practically. If I struggle with

120

depression, but God says He has given me joy, and I choose joy, I declare joy, but then still act depressed, what am I? Joyful or depressed? Conversely, if I choose to act with joy (in faith) then what am I joyful or depressed?

Now I am not saying to *fake* it, I am saying to *faith* it. Act on what you know, not what you feel! This is how you pull what you know into existence. It is what I call putting a demand on the promises of God. In the next chapter, I will talk more about your power to cause a shift in your paradigm and predetermine what your encounters will be like. But for now, let's remember that our actions prove what we say we believe. This is the point of James chapter 2. If we only speak about what we believe, but our actions never prove it, then what is the point of believing to begin with? Faith alone never saved anyone (James 2:14).

> *"So then faith that doesn't involve action is phony." (James 2:17 The Passion Translation)*

The choosing and declaring is just pumping me up for the doing. It is my pep talk. It is where I talk myself into doing the right thing, despite what I feel or think. Remember, at this point, I have already worked all that out. Now it is time to stop circling the mountain of emotions and move on. We do that through action.

If you constantly find yourself saying what you want to do or who you want to be, but you never act on what you say, then you find yourself frustrated and discouraged. You see glimpses of your potential and the potential of what you could do, but because you don't act upon it, you quickly forget. The Bible says that those people are deceived and will never come into the full blessings that are due them.

> *"But be doers of the word, and not hearers only, deceiving yourselves. For if anyone is a hearer of the word and not a doer, he is like a man observing his natural face in a mirror; for he observes himself, goes away, and immediately forgets what kind of man he was. But he who looks into the perfect law of liberty and continues in it, and is not a forgetful hearer but a doer of the work, this one will be blessed in what he does." (James 1:22-25 NKJV)*

Our action is where we partner with God in manifesting what He gave on the cross. There is not a thing in your life that His blood did not cover, heal, restore, redeem, cleanse, renew. It is all established, but it is on you to pull that establishment into your reality!

IN SUMMARY

This whole process removes variables from our lives. Instead of living life shifting back and forth, victimized by the constant stimuli of life, our emotions, our thoughts, our relationships, our politics, and so on, we get to settle on truth.

Remember, God is not shifting like the shadows, in Him there is no variation. "There is no shadow of turning with Thee!" (James 1:17).

This process takes practice, but consider the freedom and authority that you will live in once you establish that you know who you are and where you stand in every circumstance.

When Jesus gave what we call "The Great Commission," He follows by saying:

> *"And these signs will follow those who believe: In My name they will cast out demons; they will speak with new tongues; they will take up serpents; and if they drink anything deadly, it will by no means hurt them; they will lay hands on the sick, and they will recover."*
> *(Mark 16:17&18 NKJV)*

Read this verse in the context of what we have learned in this chapter. We will cast out every foul thought, emotion, and behavior and we will speak with a new message about ourselves and others (new tongues). We will grab hold of anger, depression, rejection, fear, pride, offense, etc. (serpents) and we will handle them. Though we live in a poisonous world, we will not be poisoned!

I can't help but recall in Acts 28 when a deadly "viper" latched on to Paul's hand on the island of Malta, and the Bible says that he shook it off and cast it into the fire. The natives were all expecting him to swell up and die, but instead, there was absolutely no effect of the bite! He was bitten and poisoned, "the natives saw the creature hanging from his hand" (verse 4), but with great authority and confidence, he simply shook it off. No impact, no fear, no fret, no worry. Absolutely unaffected physically or emotionally! Can you imagine having such authority? You should, because it is the authority of God that we should shake off the jaws and poison of this world and refuse to allow ourselves to be poisoned or affected by them. Learn to draw in the sand in the midst of hype. Doodle for a bit and create some space to choose your responses. Take authority to navigate your life and don't deviate from what you know and start "Enforcing YOU!"

Prayer Practice:
I thank You, God, for giving me power and authority to widen the gap in my mind. I stand on the authority You have given me to take hold of my emotions and thoughts and navigate them towards wholeness and health. Thank You for teaching me to harness my emotions and intentionally process how I want to deal with them. I recognize Your voice in that process and I thank You for shifting my paradigm because I have chosen Your truths. I choose You, I set my mind on You, I have decided on You, and I declare You as God in my life. I pray that I live intentionally and that I choose You in every response. I shake off the serpents of the world and am not poisoned by them. The world does not infect nor affect me. I am only infected and affected by Your love. I am not a victim and I do not live my life in reaction, instead I am calm and intentional. In Jesus' name I pray, amen.

Enforcing You

Passage:

"Finally, brethren, whatever things are true, whatever things are noble, whatever things are just, whatever things are pure, whatever things are lovely, whatever things are of good report, if there is any virtue and if there is anything praiseworthy—meditate on these things." (Phil. 4:8 NKJV)

Declaration:

I declare that my mind is fixed on the kingdom. That I will only focus on things that are true, noble, just, pure, lovely, and of good report. I watch for things that are praiseworthy, and I meditate on those things. Things that don't matter do not distract me, but I declare that God has given me eyes to see what is valuable and true. I rejoice in You, Father, and the gift of kingdom perspective, and I shift my mind in line with Yours and take authority to navigate my thoughts into Your ways and Your truths.

Self-reconciliation:

[Say your name], your mind has been purified by the power of the Holy Spirit and you only think about kingdom things. You are fixed on that which is true, noble, just, pure, lovely and of good report. I take the authority given to me by Jesus over my mind and declare that you are in line with the thoughts of God.

125

I speak praises over you and declare that you are filled with praiseworthy thoughts and a praiseworthy attitude. I rebuke anything foul that would plague this mind and declare a hedge of protection around it!

Passage:

"But seek first the kingdom of God and His righteousness, and all these things shall be added to you." (Matthew 6:33 NKJV)

Declaration:

I declare Your truth that as I seek You first in all that I do, along with Your character, Your ways, and Your person, everything else will fall into place. In fact, I declare that the blessings of the kingdom will be multiplied and poured out upon me. I thank You, God, for the promise that you have made and declare that because I seek You first, there is increase in my life.

Self-reconciliation:

[Say your name], you are having kingdom riches added to your life because you are seeking God first in all your ways. I speak undivided attention over your heart and mind and declare that you are solely focused on seeking Him first in all you do. You do not look left or right; you stare into His face and His ways. His character is your standard in all things.

Passage:
"Be still, and know that I am God;"
(Psalm 46:10 NKJV)

Declaration:
I declare that there is not stillness found like the stillness found in You. I receive the rest and quietness that only You can bring to my heart and I thank You for the clarity and simplicity that You release. I declare that as I know You, so I find myself and who I am. In Your person, I find the REAL me!

Self-reconciliation:
[Say your name], I speak the rest of God over your heart and mind. You are still in His presence and you find confidence in His pocket. In that space, there is no wavering, no anxiety, and no conflict, but only peace. You are at peace in the knowledge of who He is despite what is around you. There is confidence rising in you as you settle on the knowledge of God and who He is. As you know Him, so you also know the real you and the fullest potential of your God-design!

127

Passage:

"Trust in the Lord with all your heart,
And lean not on your own understanding;
In all your ways acknowledge Him,
And He shall direct your paths."
(Proverbs 3:5-6 NKJV)

Declaration:

I thank You, Lord, that as I trust You with my whole
heart, my paths become more and more clear and
secure. I lean into You, God; I acknowledge Your ways
and all You do. I rebuke any distraction that would
keep me from trusting only in You. I silence the voice
of doubt and I release Your voice that is sure. There is
no voice like Yours and in hearing You, I find myself
on a sure path.

Self-reconciliation:

[Say your name], your heart has been taken over by
the Holy Spirit and you trust Him with your whole
heart. Your mind has been consumed by the mind of
Christ and you rely on His wisdom. You are mindful
of God in every moment of every day and declare
that not a second goes by that you are not aware of
His love. You will walk through life with confidence
because you know God directs your path.

Passage:

"Now may the God of hope fill you with all joy and peace in believing, that you may abound in hope by the power of the Holy Spirit." (Romans 15:13 NKJV)

————————————

Declaration:

God, I declare that You have filled me with hope, joy, and peace. You have given me faith to believe and I receive that fullness. You are causing me to abound in hope because Your Holy Spirit lives within me and stirs me up for more. I agree with You God, I am walking empowered to be hopeful in all things!

————————————

Self-reconciliation:

[Say your name], because of the Holy Spirit, you are empowered to walk in hope. You have the faith to believe, therefore you experience the fullness of joy and peace and you are abounding in hope, despite your circumstances.

Chapter Seven
Putting a Demand on Your Design

Reflect for a moment on chapter 4, when we talked about reversing the cycle. This whole book has been about learning the pattern of how a paradigm is developed, recognizing your power to change it, and most importantly, learning how to change it. Chapter 4 introduced you to the idea of changing that pattern and chapters 5 and 6 walked you through how to begin changing the pattern. Now, I want you to see that the authority you have been practicing has the power to really predetermine how you live.

That's right! I have the ability to predetermine what my tomorrow will look like based on where I set my mind. Remember, my core beliefs ultimately predetermine all my interactions, perceptions, and perspectives. They predetermine how I will respond, how I choose to feel, what I am thinking, and who I want to be in any moment. That said, what belief I choose to set my mind on ultimately will navigate what life I will live. Now, many of you are reading this and thinking, "We can't control what happens around us; whether or not we do or don't get a job, whether or not we get into a car accident, whether or not someone lives or dies." To some degree you are right, however, the problem with that thinking is that you have limited the definition of your life to your circumstances and your reality. And remember, circumstances do not define who you are, and your reality does not necessarily equal truth. These are simply worldly experiences that threaten to define who you are in a moment. You must be aware of this! Your determination of truth can and will change the way you act and ultimately can and will shift your paradigm. But you must be confident in what you believe! When you are not confident, you will waver in moments of tense, high-emotion circumstances. This is what James calls a double-minded man who ultimately becomes unstable in all his ways.

STOP THE WAVERING

> " ...for he who doubts is like a wave of the sea driven and tossed by the wind. For let not that man suppose that he will receive anything from the Lord; he is a double-minded man, unstable in all his ways."
> (James 1:6-8 NKJV)

The word "doubt" in the Greek language denotes the idea of being at variance with one's self or to hesitate. It is often translated into the word "waver," which gives me the visual of something shifting back and forth. Hence the description of "a wave being tossed by the wind." Ugh, I can relate to that! When I am not firmly fixed, not confident in what I believe in a moment; when my reality is screaming, "YOU SHOULD BE AFRAID, YOU'RE NOT GOOD ENOUGH, SMART ENOUGH, READY ENOUGH..." "YOU'RE INADEQUATE, TOO LATE, TOO SHORT, TOO TALL..." or "THIS IS IMPOSSIBLE," "THAT COULD NEVER HAPPEN," OR "YOUR DREAM IS UNREALISTIC..." This is when the voice of my emotions, my thoughts, my circumstances, my past, and my relationships becomes like the wind... blowing me this way and that! C'mon now, we all experience this. I am not talking about never experiencing it, I am talking about operating in victory despite what we are experiencing.

This same passage in The Passion Translation says it this way:

> *"Just make sure you ask empowered by confident faith without doubting that you will receive. For the ambivalent person believes one minute and doubts the next. Being undecided makes you become like the rough seas driven and tossed by the wind. You're up one minute and tossed down the next. When you are half-hearted and wavering, it leaves you unstable. Can you really expect to receive anything from the Lord when you're in that condition?" (James 1:6-8)*

What an incredible translation that appropriately captures what I am trying to say. The word ambivalent means "having mixed feelings or contradictory ideas." Some synonyms are "uncertain, unsure, indecisive, inconclusive, irresolute, unresolved..." there are several more, and one of them is the phrase "in two minds." WOW! Yes, that nails it for me. I struggle with being in two minds... the mind of my flesh, and the mind of the Spirit. Moreover, the one I exercise the most is the one that becomes most dominant! This is why the Enforcing YOU sections of this book are imperative to your ability to stand firm, resolute, and unwavering in times of great winds.

Our stability hinges on the confidence we have in what we believe. There is nothing worse than being unsure of what to think or believe. The Word must be the anchor that keeps you fixed in the midst of instability. Just because your life is unstable, doesn't mean you have to be unstable!

YOUR RIGHTS

When you are confident in and fixed on who you are, God's truth will cause you to want to put a demand on truth for your life. It is one thing to have an understanding of what is due you and what your life could and should look like, but stepping into your right to be bold enough to put a demand on that truth is a whole other battle. I have worked with many clients and watched them shift from personal, fleshly emotions to a righteous, spiritual unction to fight for their God-design. This is the difference between what you want or think you deserve versus what God wants and what you are designed for. When you know that you know that you are designed for something, the tenacity that rises up is different than the emotion of anger, defeat, discouragement, or disappointment. Instead, it is the unction of the Holy Spirit that rises up and gives you the passion to fight for what you know is already established in the spirit. It is only by practicing the Word of God that you will grow in your confidence of who you are and what your design includes.

Many of us have settled for less than best. We hear the Word and we know the Word, but we have allowed our realities to deceive and exhaust us. It is time that we rise up and put a demand on God's design for our lives. Put your hand out and touch the hem of Jesus and demand His truth for you to flow into your life!

MARK 5

In Mark 5 we learn the story of a woman who had an issue with blood. Let's discuss her reality for a moment so you can grasp the risk of her actions. The Bible says that the woman had a problem that involved blood for twelve years. Not only that, she had been to many doctors and spent lots of money, yet her condition only grew worse. In fact, the Bible says she "spent all that she had." She was out of resources, at her wits' end, and there was nothing left she could do. Many of us can relate to that feeling. The feeling of doing all the right things, yet our condition just gets worse and worse until we throw up our hands and give up. Now, just to expound on the emotional side of this, consider that during those times, culturally, women who were bleeding were not allowed to touch people or be touched by other people. In fact, when someone in that condition was in the midst of the crowd, they were required to yell continuously, "Unclean, unclean!" Can you only imagine? When you feel like giving up and things are hard, consider what comforts you find in those moments? Typically, most of us run to other people. We rely on the relationships in our lives to soothe our aching hearts in times of discouragement. We ask for prayer or we want hands laid on us. We want a hug or a smile. Something, *anything* that will warm our hearts and bring a hint of hope into our situation.

In thinking about this, can you connect with the desperation that was in this woman's heart? Think of the beat down of life she was experiencing. It is hard enough for us to be confident when we feel confident; it is another to be confident when we don't feel confident. There is a difference between feeling confident and being confident; and remember, it is how we act—what we do—that proves what is true. You can feel confident, but if you don't DO confidence, then what is true about you? Conversely, you can feel unconfident, but if you do confidence, then what is true about you? I heard it once said that we need to learn how to "Do it afraid." It is not about getting rid of your fear or lack of confidence, it is about doing it anyway in the face of those things!

The woman with the issue of blood was faced with two possible realities: one based on her system and experiences, and one based on what she knew about truth. In a single moment, she had to choose, "Which one will I act upon?" "What do I want to believe?" Let's take that thought process a little deeper and make it more raw: "Am I worth truth?" "Am I worth healing?" "Am I significant enough that in the midst of this crowd, Jesus will take notice of me?"

So, where did this woman's confidence come from to act on truth? I have to believe that she was sure of Jesus's ability to heal her. Moreover, in the midst of her discouragement, there was something inside that told her that she was worth His healing. Let's read it and watch how her belief actually predetermined her encounter with Jesus and ultimately the paradigm she would live from that moment on. I will emphasize the key statement to ensure that you see how her core belief was the determining factor of her outcome.

> *"Now a certain woman had a flow of blood for twelve years, and had suffered many things from many physicians. She had spent all that she had and was no better, but rather grew worse. When she heard about Jesus, she came behind Him in the crowd and touched His garment.* ***For she said, 'If only I may touch His clothes, I shall be made well.'***

> *Immediately the fountain of her blood was dried up, and she felt in her body that she was healed of the affliction." (Mark 5:25-29 NKJV)*

The statement she made was said before she touched Jesus. Let's look at verses 28 and 29 in a couple of other versions. I want to make sure you get this!

> *"Woman (to herself): Even if all I touch are His clothes, I know I will be healed.*

> *"As soon as her fingers brushed His cloak, the bleeding stopped. She could feel that she was whole again." (The Voice Translation)*

> *"For she kept saying to herself, 'If only I could touch his clothes, I know I will be healed.' As soon as her hand touched him, her bleeding immediately stopped! She knew it, for she could feel her body instantly being healed of her disease!" (The Passion Translation)*

This woman wasn't messing around. She wasn't wishy washy or wavering in her mind. She didn't just *wish* for healing; she had decided to believe that Jesus was who she had heard He was. He was Healer, Restorer, Deliverer, Rescuer, and a source of Hope. He was exactly what she needed, and she decided to be sure of it. I have no doubt she struggled in her emotions in that moment of having to push through that crowd. We too must push through the noisy voices and obstacles to get what is rightfully ours! The Passion Translation says in verse 27: *"When she heard about Jesus' healing power, she pushed through the crowd and came up from behind him and touched his prayer shawl."*

Many versions say that the crowd thronged about Him. This means there were multitudes of people without any sense of order. Doesn't that aptly represent our lives sometimes? It paints a picture of the craziness we often have to navigate and push through? It can be exhausting. Not only the crowd, but also keep in mind this woman's condition. She was bleeding. No doubt she lived a life of physical fatigue. It would not have been easy for her to push through in that condition, especially without touching anyone else or being touched. Yet, she did. Interesting to note that when we see it written that "she came up" or "she came behind," the word "came" or "come" metaphorically in the Greek language means to be established, or to become known. That is exactly what happened. Her kingdom establishment was brought into existence. Why? How? Because she decided, and then she acted on her decision, thus pulling truth into her reality.

This woman had a belief that she spoke to herself. "I will be healed," "I shall be healed." Not "Maybe" or "I might" or "I hope." It started in her mind, not in her experience, her system, nor her reality. Her core belief actually navigated her encounter with Jesus! Hear me on this, there are times when our encounter with Jesus affects how or what we believe, but to the same degree, what and how we believe about Him will greatly affect how we encounter Him! I minister to many people and it is crazy how many times people have predetermined what they believe about how Jesus can work, thus putting a limit on how He shows up.

Let's read the rest of the passage about the woman and her encounter with Jesus.

> *"And Jesus, immediately knowing in Himself that power had gone out of Him, turned around in the crowd and said, 'Who touched My clothes?'*
>
> *"But His disciples said to Him, 'You see the multitude thronging You, and You say, 'Who touched Me?''*
>
> *"And He looked around to see her who had done this thing. But the woman, fearing and trembling, knowing what had happened to her, came and fell down before Him and told Him the whole truth. And He said to her, 'Daughter, your faith has made you well. Go in peace, and be healed of your affliction.'"*
> *(Mark 5:30-34 NKJV)*

In that moment, the woman "became known." Her existence was established by her action of coming to Jesus. This is not to say that God didn't already know her, because He definitely did, it is to say that her actions manifested that truth. Again, she put a demand on the truth of her existence. Remember, if you believe you are non-existent, you will act non-existent, and that will teach and train people to treat you that way, thus non-existence will become your paradigm. I really want you to understand your power to change your paradigm by changing your beliefs about YOU!

Jesus confirms what shifted her reality of affliction into wholeness. Remember, your system + your experience + Jesus has to equal a shift. But it started in faith. Jesus said, "Your faith has healed you!" The word "faith" comes from the Greek word "pistis." It means conviction of a truth, or strong belief. The root word means "to be persuaded, to trust, have confidence or be confident." This brings us back to the very beginning of this chapter! See? I am not just making up things to write; I am not that smart! This is all revealed to me through His Word.

FIGHT FOR YOUR FREEDOM

Bottom line, this woman's belief predetermined her outcome. Her faith literally empowered her to push past all that stood between her and her healing and place her hand on His cloak. Her faith pulled on His power, bringing it into her reality. This was her design: to walk in restoration, wholeness, and healing of all that afflicted her, and to walk in freedom, living abundantly. Don't see this as just physical healing; there is so much more here for you to receive. Don't miss the message that God has in mind for YOU. Many of us have had our own issues for twelve years (or longer) that have impacted the way we deal with society. But GOD! When we pull God's virtue into our lives, our paradigm has to change.

I implore you to go after more. Know what is yours and put a demand on it. Don't settle for less than His design for you. Don't settle in your afflictions: physical, emotional, or relational. Instead, set your mind on what God says and press through your "crowd" of voices to get it. The word "touch" in this passage (when she touched His cloak), in the Greek language means "to attach oneself to." That is what I am talking about. Attach yourself to truth, be fixed, anchored, resolute, and stubborn for it and don't stop at anything less!

Prayer Practice:
I am confident in who You are and what You have promised. I speak against any wavering that makes my head spin, and I plant my thoughts on You. There is no more wavering, only assuredness in Your love. I seek You first in all things and I trust You to handle the "things." There is no rock like You! I rise up in confidence and fight for what I know to be true. I recognize and press into what You have said. Thank You for empowering me and giving me the authority to press past the crowdedness of life and cling to Your hem. I believe You, God, that You have power and virtue readily available daily for me to take. I reach out my hand and take hold of Your cloak. I receive Your goodness and the promises that come with it. In Jesus' name I pray, amen.

Enforcing You

Passage:
"This hope we have as an anchor of the soul, both sure and steadfast"
(Hebrews 6:19 NKJV)

Declaration:

God, I declare that You are my anchor! I attach my soul to Yours and I look to You as my source for all things. I thank You that YOU are the hope that I cling to and that because of You, I am anchored to truth and I am sure and steadfast in all things.

Self-reconciliation:

[Say your name], you are anchored to truth by the blood of Jesus. He holds you to His truth and therefore you are sure and steadfast in all things. I speak to your soul and declare that your only anchor in life is found in Christ. Be stable, tenacious, and sure of who you are!

Passage:
"Therefore do not cast away your confidence, which has great reward. For you have need of endurance, so that after you have done the will of God, you may receive the promise..." (Hebrews 10:35-36 NKJV)

Declaration:

I declare that You are a God in whom I can be confident. When You say something, You mean it. You are not like man and You do not lie, but rather in You, I find the promises of life. Because I trust in You, I will run with confidence, knowing that my God is faithful. I will do Your will and not mine because I know that Your will leads me to Your promises.

Self-reconciliation:

[Say your name], there is one thing you are sure of and that is that God is true and faithful. All His ways are best for you and I speak against any doubt that might cause you to cast off His truth. Endurance is your strength because you know who holds your life and you are fixed on the will of God. I declare that you receive His promises and seek His will in all things. Open your heart, open your mind, open your hands, and receive the full reward of His promises!

Passage:

"Therefore we also, since we are surrounded by so great a cloud of witnesses, let us lay aside every weight, and the sin which so easily ensnares us, and let us run with endurance the race that is set before us, looking unto Jesus, the author and finisher of our faith..." (Hebrews 12:1-2 NKJV)

Declaration:

I thank You, God, that You have given examples through Your Word of so many who pressed into Your sovereignty and will for their lives. Your Word reminds me and empowers me to throw off any obstacle that would stand in the path of my race. I set my eyes on You and declare that You alone are the Author who started my story, and I declare that You are the Finisher who will finish my story.

Self-reconciliation:

[Say your name], remember the track record that God has with those He loves. Remember the track record that He has with you. He has never started something that He has not finished, and He has never left you alone. I declare that every sin that seeks to strangle you is broken in Jesus's name. Look to Him, be fixed on Him, and reject any other thing that tries to author the moments of your life. Rest in Him as He navigates you into His best.

Passage:

"...because God is your confidence in times of crisis, keeping your heart at rest in every situation."
(Proverbs 3:26 The Passion Translation)

145

Declaration:

God, You are my confidence at all times. In times of trouble, I declare that You keep my heart at rest and that I am in a constancy of peace because I am anchored to Your love.

Self-reconciliation:

[Say your name], you are confident in your troubles because you are confident in God. Your heart is at rest in every moment because you settle yourself in His love.

Passage:

"Confidence and strength flood the hearts of the lovers of God who live in awe of him, and their devotion provides their children with a place of shelter and security."
(Proverbs 14:26 The Passion Translation)

Declaration:

I declare that my heart is flooded, overtaken, consumed, and overwhelmed by Your confidence and strength because I love You and I live my life in awe of You. My devotion provides all those around me and future generations safety and security. I declare that You are our safe place today, tomorrow, and forever.

Self-reconciliation:

[Say your name], your heart is full of confidence and strength because of your love for God. He is overwhelming you with His fullness and your heart is swelling up with goodness. You are in awe of Him and nothing compares to Him. You are wholly devoted, and I declare that any distraction that might cause division in your heart is shattered in Jesus' name. Your devotion has released shelter and security in the lives of your children and generations to come.

Chapter Eight
This is Me!

I want to reflect back to the introduction, where I mentioned that this entire book was inspired by a women's conference that I spoke at entitled "This is Me," after the theme song from the movie *The Greatest Showman*.

I think *The Greatest Showman* inspired so many people because of its theme of being who you are and doing what you love without any shame. The thought of being willing to go against the grain and the voices of the world and challenge status quo no doubt stirs up something in each of us.

But the song "This is Me" was particularly impactful and won the Golden Globe Award for Best Original Song. I believe that the song was a hit because it gives permission to be proud of who you are and the way you were created. The song declares with boldness in the chorus that there is no need to apologize for who you are and the way that you are designed. That you are stepping onto the scene because you know there is indeed a place for you; that you have purpose and that you matter to the world just as you are.

> *Look out 'cause here I come*
> *And I'm marching on to the beat I drum*
> *I'm not scared to be seen*
> *I make no apologies, this is me*

My translation: World, you better watch out because I have discovered who I am and the power that my design holds. I have decided that I am taking authority; that I am the head and not the tail. I have decided to be fearless and confident and I am no longer making excuses. I don't have to justify who I am or the way I am designed. You can take it or leave it. It no longer matters to me because I am beating to the drum of the Holy Spirit; He sets my pace. Either way I am not changing or settling for less than ME! This is my God-design and I will not let you steal it, dampen it, nor shame it!

This song declares more than just "I'm OK with who I am." This is a *celebration* of who we are. It is more than just having the knowledge to say the right words; it is a boasting of the heart. It is an overflow of what the singer has chosen to believe, and it is a declaration to take action.

If you have seen the movie, you know that this song carries a whole new level of impact in that it is being sung by people who were typically laughed at and ridiculed for the way they were born. Mockery was their norm. A bearded woman, a "midget," a bi-racial woman, their very creation, their God-design was being shamed, and they were considered "freaks of nature."

They wrestled their whole lives with the looks, the stares, and the perceptions of those around them. That was the only system they knew, and it was what they had always experienced. When they are first introduced in the movie, we see that they have "settled into" their system and experience. The perception of others had become their paradigm and shaped their core beliefs about who they were and their value in society! They had been molded by society.

But then... a man (played by Hugh Jackman) entered into their lives and took their greatest places of shame and their point of vulnerability and shone a light on it. He connects with them because of their weaknesses for the purpose of putting them on a stage, in the spotlights. It kind of sounds cruel if you didn't know his heart. He doesn't see them the way the world does. He sees their beauty and it is his care of them, his love for them, and his belief in them that filled them with hope and courage. They saw something in the way he looked at them that they didn't see in the eyes of the world. Ultimately, they shift from seeing themselves through the eyes of those around them and choose to believe what the man saw. They begin to delight in who they are, and they embrace their creation; their God-design!

You see, simply believing one man who saw something different changed their core belief about who they were. The world missed it, but he saw it.

Of course, you know where I am going with this. Hugh Jackman's character in a lot of ways represented a "God-like" figure in the movie. He came in and capitalized on their greatest weakness and turned them into their greatest strengths!

"But he said to me, 'My grace is sufficient for you, for my power is made perfect in weakness.' Therefore I will boast all the more gladly about my weaknesses, so that Christ's power may rest on me. That is why, for Christ's sake, I delight in weaknesses, in insults, in hardships, in persecutions, in difficulties. For when I am weak, then I am strong." (2 Cor. 12:9-11 NKJV)

This story sounds a lot like Jesus with the woman at the well. He connected with her in her greatest point of shame and shifted the way she viewed herself. What she believed about herself was shifted when Jesus was added to her equation. Ultimately, He put her "on the stage" of Samaria just like what happened in the movie! She moved from being influenced by the world to influencing the world.

Changing how we see ourselves starts with what we choose to believe. It goes far beyond our abilities, gifts, or talents. I heard it once said that your gifts will get you to "the top," but it is your character that keeps you there. The people in *The Greatest Showman* all had talents, but that wasn't enough to cause them to make changes around them; they needed a change of mind. It wasn't just about their gifts; it was about their belief system. That is the change that ultimately caused an entire paradigm shift...not just in their lives, but also in the lives of many others! They became the influencers instead of the influenced. This is a great example to you and me, as believers in Christ. If you want to influence the world, however, you must start by believing what God says about you!

SING YOUR PRAISES

I can't help but think of Paul and Silas in Acts 16. They were thrown into prison for taking a stand for what they believed. While in jail, they chose to respond to their truth versus their reality. Their reality gave no reason to praise, but their truth was so cemented into their hearts that they couldn't help but sing! Their reality had them in chains, but their truth was celebrating freedom. There were no chains that could steal what Jesus had given them. Praise was a part of their design and they refused to let a circumstance steal it or rewrite it. By engaging in what they believed, they put a demand on what was true. They pulled Jesus into the equation and the ground started shaking and quaking. They literally caused a shift in the atmosphere that ultimately pulled the truth of their freedom into their reality and their prison doors swung wide open. O man, I could preach on this all day long! But there's more! Not only were their doors opened, but all the prison doors were opened. More importantly, hearts were saved, and freedom was had by all in the natural and the spirit.

This is just another example of how the declaration of truth will cause a shift in your life and the lives of those around you. If you do nothing else, learn to sing! Sing the praises of God and watch how it changes the atmosphere within and without. Learn to celebrate your design and who you are. Go ahead, boast about your creation. Look in the mirror and declare to yourself:

> *I am child of God. Look out devil because here I come, and I am marching to the beat of the Holy Spirit. He sets my pace and He keeps my beat. I am not scared, I am not broken, I am not weak, and I am not done! Today AND tomorrow, I am coming onto the scene... you better run cause here I come, THIS IS ME!*

I will let that be your final prayer practice!

Enforcing You

Passage:

"For the Lord God will help Me;
Therefore I will not be disgraced;
Therefore I have set My face like a flint,
And I know that I will not be ashamed."
(Isaiah 50:7 NKJV)

Declaration

God, I thank You that Your Word says You will help
me; not You might or maybe, but You WILL. I rejoice
in that truth and respond accordingly. I am confident
that I will not be disgraced or shamed; I will be
upheld by Your hand. For this reason, I am fixed on
You. I set my face like flint on Your smile and I
saturate myself in Your love.

Self-reconciliation

[Say your name], God will help you. In this, you are
confident. You have no fear of being shamed or
disgraced and therefore, your face is like flint. You
are satisfied and confident in His love!

Passage:
"I will greatly rejoice in the Lord,
My soul shall be joyful in my God;
For He has clothed me with the garments of
salvation,
He has covered me with the robe of righteousness,
As a bridegroom decks himself with ornaments,
And us a bride adorns herself with her jewels."
(Isaiah 61:10 NKJV)

Declaration:
I declare that I am clothed in the fullness of Your
garments. I am covered by Your love and Your
anointing adorns me. Your brilliance is upon me and
I am dressed and ready to go! I rejoice GREATLY, a
"big rejoice" is my theme and my soul is content in
You. My soul is joyful always and I boast in You
because I am confident in Your provision and
covering.

Self-reconciliation:
[Say your name], you are covered by the love of God.
You are not naked or unprepared. His anointing has
slathered a covering on you that adorns you like the
most precious jewels. When people look at you, they
see unexplainable confidence and readiness. The joy
of the Lord is your strength, and I declare a heart of
joy over you always.

Passage:

"Be strong and of good courage, do not fear nor be afraid of them; for the Lord your God, He is the One who goes with you. He will not leave you nor forsake you." (Deut. 31:6 NKJV)

Declaration

I declare that I am strong! I declare that I am courageous! I declare that I am not afraid! I declare that God is my God! I declare that God is with me! I declare that God never leaves me! I declare that I am not forsaken!

Self-reconciliation

[Say your name], I declare that you are strong! I declare that you are courageous! I declare that you are not afraid! I declare that God is your God! I declare that God is with you! I declare that God never leaves you! I declare that you are not forsaken!

Passage:

"He gives power to the weak,
And to those who have no might He increases strength." (Is. 40:29 NKJV)

Declaration

I declare that I have been given power and strength. I rejoice that in times of weakness, I have Your strength and power to carry me through.

157

Self-reconciliation

[Say your name], you are filled with the power and strength of God. I declare that His strength is increasing in you daily, and that even where you feel weak, He is empowering you.

Passage:

"And I find that the strength of Christ's explosive power infuses me to conquer every difficulty."
(Phil. 4:13 The Passion Translation)

Declaration:

I declare God's explosive power in my life. I declare that I am infused with the Holy Spirit to conquer all things. I declare victory in difficulties. I declare that because You conquered the grave, I am a conqueror!

Self-reconciliation

[Say your name], I declare God's explosive power in your life. I declare that you are infused with the Holy Spirit to conquer all things. I declare that you walk in victory in difficulties. I declare that in Christ, you are a conqueror!

Conclusion

I think that sometimes we hyper-spiritualize, overthink, and complicate things to the point that they often seem unattainable. I had a few spiritually mature (older) people read this manuscript as I was finishing it up, and they all came back saying, "I wish I would have read this years ago." The consensus was that even though they had knowledge of most of the concepts presented, they had never heard it so "simply and practically" taught.

It was my desire for this book to be short, simple, and practical. I have met with so many people over the years who have had so much biblical knowledge and understanding of "Christianity," yet they are not walking in the fullness of their design. They are frustrated, discouraged, and disappointed. Ultimately that leads to settling for or just accepting that, "This must be it; as good as it gets!"

Some of you have read this and thought the same, while some of you may be thinking, "I already knew all of that." And that's OK! Just don't close your mind to learning more. Remember the greatest threat to learning is our existing knowledge. I implore you to remain stayed on the truth that says, "There is more for you!"

Many of us have settled for learning the basics in math or music or reading and writing. We have probably even made statements like, "That just isn't my strength" and we learned just enough to get through school or just enough to help us at our jobs. But what if you could master those subjects? Now, I am not saying that you want to, I am just proposing a mindset shift from *I can't* to *I could*. I am proposing the possibility of having MORE!

As you close this book, let me ask you these questions:

1. Are you living your life to your fullest potential? If yes, are you sure? How do you know that you're sure? If not, why not?
2. Is there an area in your life where you feel victimized, like you have no control, or "there's nothing you can do about it?"
3. Do you wake up every day confident in your ability to navigate how you will end your day?
4. Are you living the way you want to live?
5. Have you become who you want be?

One of my driving motivations for pressing on toward God's best for me is that I do not want to reach the end of my life, look back, and have regrets. I don't want to think, "What if I could have or what if I would have..." God has ordained all the days of my life that I would live them to the fullest and with great satisfaction. I am determined to believe Him and step into my authority to put a demand on all He has designed. How about you?

LISA SCHWARZ

Enforcing purpose

Lisa Schwarz is a national speaker, published author, Certified Biblical Counselor, Professional Life Coach, Brain Health Coach, and Founder/CEO of Crazy8 Ministries. She also designs and develops events, conferences, trainings and workshops for diverse settings throughout the United States. Her mantra is to enforce purpose in the lives of others.

Lisa has a powerful and effective mission that has broadened to include counseling, consulting and coaching for individuals, groups and organizations as well as a restorative housing program for men, women and their children. All of this is to reach out and equip individuals, empower people and enforce purpose in their lives through the transforming power of Jesus Christ.

Lisa also has a passion for *community* and believes in the power of unity. For this purpose, she is driven to teach, train, and inspire others within her community and desires to be a catalyst for cultivating community collaborations; *together we are better.*

Lisa is involved in various community groups within her county including:

- Faith Community Connection
- Joshua Chamber of Commerce
- Cleburne Chamber of Commerce
- Burleson Chamber of Commerce
- Burleson Ministerial Alliance

She founded the Burleson Empowerment Project, serves as a board member for the Cleburne Area Chamber of Commerce, is on the advisory board of Couch & Russell Financial Group, serves as a founding member of the Cleburne Chamber of Commerce Women's Leadership Initiative and as well as the Cleburne Charity Community Coordination. She is the secretary for the Burleson Character Council and is a part of the Community Health Needs Assessment Advisory Team for Texas Health Huguley Hospital. She also founded the Crazy8 Ministries' City on a Hill Festival held annually in Burleson, TX.

She and her husband, Brad, reside in Texas and have six wonderful children, a daughter-in-law, and a son-in-law.

Made in the USA
Las Vegas, NV
05 December 2021